THE

DIFFERENCE

10 STEPS TO WRITING
A BOOK THAT MATTERS

Angela E. Lauria

Editing:
Kate Makled

Interior Design:
John H. Matthews, bluebullseye.com

Author's Photo Courtesy Of:
John H. Matthews, jhmatthews.com

For Brooke, who saw through my BS from day one and held the space for me to create a life I love instead of one I was begrudgingly willing to settle for. Thank you for going big.

When you find a mentor who you believe can guide you to your highest self, commit with everything you have, and be amazed by what you create.

TABLE OF CONTENTS

INTRODUCTION:
TOOK ME YEARS TO WRITE,
WILL YOU TAKE A LOOK?

Write while the heat is in you
~ Henry David Thoreau

I bet you've wanted to write a book for a long time. I bet you've had many ideas. Maybe you've even started a couple of manuscripts, and they are sitting unfinished in a drawer, or on another computer somewhere. Maybe you haven't started writing at all, because you simply aren't sure which book to start with. Yet something in you knows, You Were Born to Write a Book.

The reality is, many people *want* to have written a book, but few are called to see the process through. There are some common obstacles, sure, like writer's block, fear of failure, and not having enough time. But these are challenges every author faces. How do some people work through those concerns while others don't? What's the missing piece?

Writing a book is a major project. That said, books provide a good return on the emotional and financial investment authors make in them. It's time to learn the difference between people who say they want to write a book, and those who finish and publish one.

You're about to be introduced to some key knowledge and information that can help you make the difference you were born to make in the world. You will be able to write a book that matters. You will have something no one can take away. As an author, you craft a legacy that makes your ideas immortal.

Here's what my experience tells me: you wouldn't be reading this if you weren't meant to write a book. Most people who want to write a book don't actually seek out help and advice. If you read this book and make an ongoing effort to learn and practice what's in it, then you will know and develop everything you need to finish your first book. This could be a pivotal choice: between making the difference in the world you were born to make; or living out the frustration that your impact wasn't as big as you, in your heart, know it can and should be.

The information in this book centers around freeing your Inner Author, so you can master the key elements of preparing to write, writing, publishing, and promoting your book. Most book coaches and writing groups tend to focus on things like character development, story arc, and writing style. Maybe it's because of their appreciation for the literary arts, but I have come to know that many of the books that have a big impact in the world were not written by gifted writers following literary rules.

Have you ever heard of the *Rich Dad, Poor Dad* book series? Written by Hawaii-native and real estate investor Robert Kiyosaki, these books have made a real difference to millions of people who have adopted some of his philosophies on developing a healthy relationship with money. Kiyosaki admits to not being a great writer – he even flunked English twice in high school – but he knew he had a message people needed to hear. It's not to say good writing isn't a positive, but it's not the most important component when it comes to writing a book that makes a difference in people's lives, or even many people's lives. As Kiyosaki himself says, "There is a big difference between being a good writer and a best-selling author."

Maybe it's because the craft of writing is so complex and multilayered, but I don't think most book coaches and writing experts understand that a book that's going to change the world can't come together in an ivory tower. There's a whole universe of "stuff" that has to happen before an author can create a book that is going to have an impact. The planning and publishing stages are just as important as the writing itself, even though those parts of the process don't get as much attention.

For lots of people, just finishing a book can be tough enough. First, you have to settle on a genre and topic. Then, you have to make the time in your busy schedule to write about 200 pages on the topic. After that, you have to find a way to edit it (or hire an editor) so that there is a consistent voice, message, and story line to follow. (This last one can take months or years!) It's an intense process that can be overwhelming for most first time authors. So why does it have to be so hard?

Well, that's what we're here to talk about.

It's taken me a long time to figure out the things that you're about to learn. I've been working with authors on completing their books since 1994. From my years in the industry, I've learned that the book planning (the work you do *before* you start writing the book), and the publishing approach the author selects will play a *huge* role in building the foundation for the book – and setting the course for making its powerful impact on the world.

I think book planning, and selecting the right publishing approach, are each more significant than most people appreciate. That's not to say that writing a good book isn't important, it certainly is! But it's only one-third of the equation. The decisions you make before you get into the writing process are twice as likely to affect the outcome. And if the outcome you want is to share the lessons you have learned, and transform the pain you have experienced into real help for others that will make a difference in their lives, then these are two critical parts of the process you don't want to skip over. You've come too far, and struggled too much, to let your message go unheard.

If an author doesn't know much about how the publishing industry works, or the simple art of how a reader selects a book, then she's bound to run into problems and barriers that keep her from creating a book that makes a difference. If instead she chooses to learn to connect with the book she was born to write, then to write from a place of clarity and joy, and *most importantly*, to truly free her Inner Author – writing a book that makes a difference comes naturally with ease.

This book is *jam-packed* with this kind of insight. The best way to use it at first is to read it through once, cover-to-cover, but don't struggle to get every point or do every exercise. I want you to get an overview of how I redefine the process of writing a book to include these three focus areas (in my course I cover them in trimesters), and how each is important in its own way. Once you get that perspective, use the book as more of a reference manual. When you identify where you are stuck in your book journey, or find you are not being as effective or relaxed as you'd like, come back to the book and find the exercises and ideas that will help you improve in those areas, and work through them more readily.

It's important that you understand the knowledge in this book took years to refine, just reading it through once is not going to magically turn you into a bestselling author and massively popular TED Talk contributor. The answers to writing a book that matters are in here, but it's your job to make notes and follow up on the insights you gather when you find a section that applies to your situation.

I recommend journaling as you work through this book, and it is particularly helpful to restate some of the principles discussed in your own words so that you begin to "own" the concepts. The more you do this, the more "aha" moments you'll have – which is directly related to the probability that your book will cause "aha" moments in your readers.

It's up to you! And that's the good news.

As your guide or your book coach, I can't do your thinking and writing for you. You alone get to make the decision that you'll do what it takes to separate yourself from the throngs of people who *want to write a book*, and join the elite group of humans known as *authors*. Once you have published your first book, you'll be in this new club, *for life*.

Make this book your good luck charm. Decide that as long as you are connected to this book, you are moving closer to your goal. The quality of the connection matters! I always tell students in my Free Your Inner Author workshops that connecting means integrating the lessons into their lives as writers – whether re-reading sections that cover ground where you're struggling, doing worksheets on the topics where you lack clarity, or sharing your process with friends and loved ones who also say they want to write a book that matters. Before you know it, you will have mastered these concepts, completed a hero's journey, and have the book you've dreamed of having. But if you tuck it into a bookshelf and hope these lessons will be calcified through osmosis, I'm afraid these lessons won't have the impact you'd like for them to have.

Many people have an incomplete sense of how to learn from books. They make the mistake of reading a book and deciding they know the information in it, but they put the book down before they have actually mastered the information – as it applies to their life – and poof! The knowledge they gained – and the benefit they could have derived – from reading the book is gone. It didn't have anywhere to stick, and so the potential wisdom fades away.

Perhaps if the book were about being a smarter homeowner, or finding new volunteer opportunities around the world, it would be acceptable. But your *book* has the potential to change the world! You could be sitting on the next *Road Less Travelled* or *Seven Habits of Highly Effective People.* Your book could lead millions of people to healing, wholeness, and new life opportunities. To turn away from the ideas and tools that are in this book, before you master them will not only hurt you, it could hurt all the people whose lives your book will change. Don't make this mistake.

If there is one thing I'd like you to remember, it's this –

Don't stop to put this book on a shelf until you are actually writing your own book.

My approach to helping people write their very own book – whether it's through one-on-one coaching, in my workshops and programs, or here in this book – is different than the other solutions out there, and I'd like to explain how.

First, I consider myself to be an AUTHOR'S Coach – not a Book Coach or a Writing Expert. This is important, because I believe individuals are holistic systems – therefore you can't just direct one part of the brain or body to perform without understanding and treating the system as a whole. I named my company The Author Incubator, because we create an environment that permits and nurtures the formation and development of authors, who in turn write important books. It's not about tweaking one or two variables in your process – we adjust the entire environment to create new possibilities.

Second, as we have discussed, while I think good writing is important, it's also only one part of what makes a book *matter*. I get so frustrated when I hear about – or read on my own – a tremendously well-written book with a powerful message that isn't out in the world changing lives the way it should be.

It's not the author's fault of course, as most of the intelligence behind crafting an impactful book isn't out there for them to discover. What's worse, the little bit of information that is available is massively overshadowed by truckloads of information, programs, and support for the actual *writing*.

I host a podcast called Book Journeys Radio. Every week, I interview authors whose books have made a difference in the world. We discuss the process that has taken them from the *idea* of writing a book to holding their book in their hands. One of the things that surprises me most in those interviews is how few of them actually understood how they were able to achieve the results they achieved. It was almost as if the folks I was interviewing had just gotten lucky and won the "change the world" sweepstakes.

I was just talking about this phenomenon to Ali Cudby, a member of The Author Incubator and author of *BUSTED: The Fab Foundations Guide to Finding a Bra that Fits, Flatters and Feels Fantastic*. Ali was working as a home builder when her father died after a long illness. I met her at a seminar, and she told me her father's death had awakened her desire to create a legacy and really change women's lives.

Ali's mission was to help women discover that simply finding a bra that fits can be a foundation for building self-esteem. She didn't want to write a book that sat on a shelf, she wanted to write a book that made a difference. We worked together to craft a book that would be the cornerstone of her legacy. To make sure she wrote a book that got her authentic message to the women it could help, so she could change the world with her vision, Ali followed the 10 steps of my D.I.F.F.E.R.E.N.C.E. Process and has now helped thousands of women shift their perspective on the empowering role that well-fitting lingerie can play in a woman's whole life.

So what are those ten steps? I've analyzed hundreds of books that have made a difference and discovered they all share the same attributes of success. That's why I want to share these steps with you, because they help you ensure your book has them, too.

I call this The D.I.F.F.E.R.E.N.C.E. Process, and you can use it to write your book with authenticity, ease, and certainty that you will be effective in writing a book that matters.

D - Define your Audience.
It's a bit of a paradox, but by narrowly defining who you want to help, you exponentially increase your chances of

reaching that audience AND people beyond that audience.

I - Identify your Voice.
Agents of change have one thing in common – they don't create change from a place of force. To avoid this common temptation, it's essential they are super clear about who they are. And that's what you need to do too. So you need to establish your most authentic voice (and consequently leave both forceful and manipulative behind) before you start writing.

F - Frame your Outcome.
In Stephen Covey's, highly influential work, 7 Habits of Highly Effective People, he talks about beginning with the end in mind. He explains the principle that all things are actually created twice – there is a mental (first) creation, followed by a physical (second) creation. In order to guarantee your book will make a difference, you need to begin with the end in mind. By doing so,

you get super clear about what outcome you want for your book, right out of the gate.

F - Focus Your Author Mojo.
There are ALWAYS reasons to NOT work on your book. In order to get your book done, you need to clear your schedule to clear the path for your future. Tapping into your Author Mojo is all about being honest and authentic about what works for you, right now. Not what worked in college, what works for your sister, or what you think SHOULD work for you if only…things were different. By being honest with yourself about your work style and productivity patterns, we can create a schedule that supports *you* to reach completion.

E - Envision Your Success.
While "Framing your Outcome" is about visualizing the impact you will have in the world, "Envisioning your Success" is about clearing your mind to write the

book you were born to write, and removing the common obstacles that keep most people back.

R - Release Your Blocks.

I've said this before and you will definitely hear me say it again. The biggest mistake most first time authors make is starting their book by writing. If you skip every other part of the DIFFERENCE process, this is the one I want you to focus on. Start by writing an outline that's organic and authentic, not forced.

E - Establish your Author Feeling State.

Did you see that movie *Like Water For Chocolate?* In it, the main character cooks. The food she makes takes on the emotions she had while she was cooking it, so everyone who eats the food feels the same feelings. The same is true for your readers. Whatever emotional state you are in while you are writing will be – on some subtle level – transferred to your reader. That's why you need to write your book from a place of joy and freedom, because this energy fuels creativity and attracts more positive emotion. You want to feel, as you write, how you *think you'll feel* when the book is done.

N - Nurture your Manuscript.

You started with the end in mind by framing your outcome. But you can't stop there. Once your manuscript is complete, you need to check back in with it. Does it meet the goals you identified in your planning process? Ensure your editor, publisher, and every early reader understands what you are doing with your book, so the feedback you get from them is as relevant as possible. Make sure every adjustment is in line with your desired outcome. This may be a time to adjust or clarify your desired outcome. That's fine, but don't fall into the trap many authors do – getting sucked into other people's goals or opportunities for your book.

C - Create your Masterpiece.

How, and with whom, you publish your book will be a substantial determining factor in the impact your book can have in the world. Pick a publishing option that you are sure supports your goals.

E - Expand your Reach.

While it's essential to define the group of people you want most to help, once the book is published, you will be able to expand your reach beyond that group – but not sooner. Writing a book that makes a difference is all about doing the hard work of marketing before a word is written on the page. It's perfect for folks who don't want to have to sell or promote themselves. If you do it right, you'll expand your reach and market your book in a way that doesn't feel like you are marketing at all.

The DIFFERENCE Process is detailed – but it's simple, and proven. It breaks down each of the elements that every book that makes a difference does well, and as you work through this book, you'll see exactly, step-by-step, how you can do it too. If you follow this process, you WILL absolutely end up with a book that matters.

So here's one last thing I'd like you to do now, before delving deeper. It's a pretty easy exercise, but it's important, too. Take a moment and literally imagine your completed book in your hands right now. Don't worry about the topic of the book, or the style, or anything really – except how the book makes you *feel*. When you hold that book in your hands, in your mind's eye, see if you can find one word that crystallizes what your book needs to be in the world *for you*. What's your intention for your book?

Did you get the word? Great! Once you've got it, I'd like you to write it in some beautiful calligraphy, or use a special font and color and print it out. This is going to be the first building block of your creativity temple. More on that in chapter 6, but for now – just claim your word and give it a place of honor in your office (or wherever you write).

Listen, if you have often thought about writing a book, or if people are always telling you that you should write a book, that's not a coincidence. It's a whisper of truth from your Inner Author. Not everyone gets that whisper. You have been called, and the time to free your Inner Author is now. You don't have to wait for permission. You don't have to solve all your problems first. You don't need to have more free time. Be open to the whisper. Believe this can be done – and that it doesn't have to be hard. Make peace with your inner critic. Release the fear you are not enough, *or just write your book anyway.* Write the book you once desperately needed to read. Let your authentic voice rise to the surface. There is a special, unrepeatable brilliance in you and the world deserves to see it shine. Your book is already written, so your only job is to remove the obstacles between you and its expression. Hold your book in your hands before your write it. Open your heart to your writing muse. Know that once you are an author, your life will never be the same.

Don't give up.

You were born to make a difference.

Inside the Author Incubator:
On Fear

Q: What's the biggest fear that trips people up with they decide to write a book?

A: I've worked with dozens of authors over the past couple of decades, and no matter how experienced or successful the author is, at some point we tackle the fear of not being worthy of being an author. At some point, almost every author I've ever worked with has asked me: "Who am I to write this book?"

When this issue comes up, I tell them the same thing I'm going to tell you here. You are the perfect person to write your book, because you're the one with the desire to make a difference with your perspective. I believe, on some level, the book you are meant to bring into being already exists. Your job, should you choose to accept it, is to remove the obstacles between you and that book. That's not just some woo-woo philosophy of life. I have found, time and time again, that when authors I am working with get clear on the book they were born to write, bring that book into the world becomes easy and joyful. Struggle and writer's block seem irrelevant.

What I've seen consistently is that when an author takes the time to connect with the book they are truly meant to write, right now, the typical excuses for not starting or finishing – such as lack of time, competing priorities, or work or family obligations – melt away. How does this happen? Clearly the circumstances themselves aren't changing. So, what's different?

I have come to believe the biggest fear that trips me up is NOT the fear of failure that the "Who am I to write this book?" statement implies. Actually, it's the fear of success. It's a subtle distinction, but many authors-in-transformation fear the impact their book could have. Perhaps you have heard this famous Marianne Williamson quote:

"Our deepest fear is not that we are inadequate. Our deepest fear is that we are powerful beyond measure. It is our light, not our darkness that most frightens us. We ask ourselves, Who am I to be brilliant, gorgeous, talented, fabulous? Actually, who are you not to be? Your playing small does not serve the world. There is nothing enlightened about shrinking so that other people won't feel insecure around you. We are all meant to shine, as children do."

The DIFFERENCE Process helps authors work through the biggest fears around becoming an author, and surrounds you in a safe place to play big and let your light shine.

Have a question for The Author Incubator? Send me your ideas, comments and complaints. I want to know what you think. You can reach me at:

TheAuthorIncubator.com/contact-us

CHAPTER ONE:
I'VE GOT TWO
TICKETS TO PARADISE

Without deep suffering, menders can't possibly help the people who will later look into their eyes and ask, "Can I really be happy after living through this hell?"

~ Martha Beck, **Wild New World**

Purchased on February 10, 2007. >

If I'm So Smart, Why Can't I Lose Weight?: Tools to Get it Done

Brooke Castillo ★★★★☆ (80)

Purchased on February 10, 2007. >

Finding Your Own North Star: Claiming the Life You Were Meant to Live

Martha Beck ★★★★☆ (212)

February 10, 2007: The day I ordered these 2 books: *If I'm So Smart, Why Can't I Lose Weight?* by Brooke Castillo, and *Finding Your Own North Star* by Martha Beck.

This was the day I changed everything in my life – with a click of a button, and a commitment in my heart. I was going to get healthy and find a job I loved. Doing those two things, I thought, would fix my marriage. I'd never heard of life coaching – but I had a deep familiarity with hell, because I was living in it and I was ready to get out! I weighed 315 pounds, had a colicky 11 month old, was freshly and spectacularly fired from my dream job (the day before Christmas), and my marriage was beyond repair – yet I had no idea how to escape.

These two books were my ticket out of hell, and they are the reason I do the work I do today. I am so all-encompassingly grateful to authors Brooke Castillo and Martha Beck for beating back whatever gremlins they faced to bring me the books that introduced me to myself.

<u>Future authors take note</u>: I didn't simply spend $20 on these books. I've spent $15k – $20k with each of these authors on retreats, workshops, one-on-one coaching and certifications. And it's unlikely I'm done investing with them. The day I bought their books, I started a loyal customer relationship with them.

How many $20k clients would you need to have the business you want? 5 a year? 10?

Did you know that when you write a book that makes a difference, you create opportunities to help people far beyond a single book sale?

Most authors don't. Most first-time authors are focused on two things: sharing the information they have (or telling the story they want to tell), and making money from their book sales.

Wrong. Wrong. Wrong.

Neither of these objectives will get you money or a book that makes a difference.

What Martha and Brooke were doing, with their books, was serving their reader. They cared about me more than they cared about telling their own story. They weren't focusing on book sales, they were focusing on building a life of service – in service – to people like me who were deeply in pain.

Now if that's not a commitment you can make, then stop reading this book right now and get a refund.

Writing a book that matters is not for the weak-willed or self-indulgent. Writing a book that matters is about stepping into your own power and standing up to serve.

There are other types of books you can write. You can write a book for self-expression or as a creative outlet, and I am not judging either of those decisions. The commitment I have made for my life is to serve authors who truly want to help people who are in pain, and who are willing to get out of their own way to do it.

If you can make that commitment to your reader – to serve them first above all else – then I can teach you how to write a book that will sell, and that will attract readers who want to go deeper with you – like I have with Brooke and Martha. I will teach you how to write a book that will attract readers who will gladly hock their jewelry and take a loan to make a long-term investment in you (and themselves). That's what I did to work with Brooke and Martha, and that's what your readers will do when they come to fully believe you understand their problem, you have a solution, and you are committed to serving them through their challenge and celebrating their success when they reach their goals.

Making the Commitment to Serve

"Sure, I want to help people, but what does that mean?"

Most people believe the best way to help people is to tell them what they learned that helped them. It's logical and it seems like it would work, right?

Nopers.

Think back to the biggest changes and transformations in your life. Did they come from someone telling you: "You should do this." Or "You should do that?" Probably not.

It's easy to forget, but for most people, growth comes through confronting, and eventually solving problems. Maybe, like me, you are 315 pounds, or you have a colicky baby, or your husband tells you he wants to have sex with other people, or you get fired from your dream job – perhaps all of that happens at once if you are exceptionally lucky! But very rarely do people seek out non-fiction books about things that would be nice to know, or tell a good story.

Do me a favor. Take a break from reading this, and go look at your nightstand or book shelf, or open up your kindle app. Look at each of the non-fiction books you possess, and remember why you bought them. Sometimes it helps if you can date the purchase. I'll give you a little snap shot of my bookshelf:

BOOK	PROBLEM	TIME-FRAME
The Kindle Publishing Revolution by Ryan Deiss	I'm starting an eBook division for my business. What the hell am I doing? How can I learn more about Kindle Publishing really fast so my clients think I know what I'm talking about.	August 27 (2 weeks before I launched my first ebook offering)
Make Him Beg to Be Your Boyfriend by Michael Fiore	OMG OMG OMG I met the most amazing guy!!!! How can I get him to stick around?	Dec. 7 (21 days after I met my current partner)
Networking is Not Working by Derek Coburn	Nothing ever seems to come out of the time I spend at networking events. If I'm going to do more networking, I need to figure out how to make it worth my time.	May 15 (just after I spoke at a networking event and didn't get any business from it)
The Big Leap by Gay Hendricks	How can I bust through my current blind spots and grow my business even more?	October 26 (just as I was starting my business planning for the next year)
Mating in Captivity by Esther Perel	I'm serious thinking about getting married, but I'm worried our romantic life won't be as exciting when everything is in a place of certainty.	November 1 (just as we are heading into our first holiday season as an established couple)

Now, those are just 5 random books off my shelf. I bet you'll find a similar story on your shelf. For purposes of this exercise, only look at non-fiction books – and ignore books that were gifted to you, or that you bought on a strong recommendation, but wouldn't have gravitated to on your own.

When you do this exercise, I want you to really think about the place you were in your life when you made the purchase. Think about your frame of mind, and your feeling state. What were you worried about? What was keeping you up at night? What did you think needed to change?

There is no way to write a book that makes a difference unless you can get into the heart and soul of your reader. To have a servant's heart as a writer is to be able to place yourself into your reader's shoes and to write a book *for* them and not *to* them.

Once you reflect on your bookshelf, think about your own book. What is the problem it solves? What would be the one or two sentences your reader uses to define their problem – in their own words, like I did above? What is the book you could write to solve that problem?

Listen to me. Do not try to back into this by trying to get the reader to want what you want to write. That is not service, that's manipulation – and your readers will feel it. Even if they like your book, they won't put it into practice, because no one likes to be manipulated.

So stop.

Drop into your heart.

Imagine your ideal reader in your mind's eye, and surround them in light.

Love them like they were your best friend in the world.

And in your heart, ask them: What do you need from me?

Thinking Like Your Ideal Reader

Sandra came to me to talk about her book. She had been wounded over and over by men who would come into her life, treat her like a princess, and then walk all over her once she let her guard down. After three divorces, a broken arm from a domestic violence situation, two bankruptcies, and losing her kids in a custody battle with a much wealthier and more charming ex, she was done. She was never going to get into another relationship again – until she could learn how to make this stop.

She invested in several books, and then a workshop, and then she got a coach. The more she tried to figure out how to avoid dating men who were narcissistic and manipulative, the more her teachers pushed her to love herself. She was fine with that, but she still wanted to know: "How can I be 100% sure the next guy isn't going to turn into another nightmare?"

She wanted to know if there was a personality test or some sort of psychological evaluation she could require. She asked energy workers and experts in body language how to pick up on lying tells. She wanted to learn everything about how to read a person before she gave her heart again.

Sandra was an avid student. Very few people in the world know more about male dating behaviors and how to identify an honest man than Sandra. But in the end, Sandra realized, the answer really was self-love. It was never about judging the men she was meeting, it was about changing herself so that guys who weren't honest weren't interested in approaching her.

The more she practiced self-love, the more invisible she became to the jerks of the world. The new men who came into her orbit were honest, caring, and focused on taking care of themselves.

When she met her guy, she was so excited. She told me, she HAD to write a book about it. She had to get this story out that if you love yourself, you'll meet a great guy.

Sounds good, right?

Yeah. Nope again.

Sandra was not serving, she was bragging.

When you are single, following a string of relationships where you were clearly (in your opinion) wronged and abused, who the heck wants to hear, "Love yourself and you'll meet at great guy!"

I asked Sandra how she would have felt about that advice a couple years before she met the great guy, and she admitted she wouldn't have heard it or seen it at all – because she was too busy looking up "portable lie detector tests" and "enneagram dating match advice."

Right! She thought the problem was, "I don't know how to identify good guys from jerks." She didn't think she had a self-love problem. She loved herself plenty – which was why she was never going to date a jerk again.

So the book called *How to Love Yourself So You Meet the Right Guy* just wouldn't have addressed her problem. If Sandra really wanted to help her ideal reader, she needed to drop her whole story about the "right" answer and SERVE.

A book called *Gems & Jerks: How to Spot the Right Guys and Steer Clear of the Rest* would be the perfect book for her ideal reader. Inside, Sandra would reveal the truth – that this problem goes away when you love yourself. But on the cover and the marketing copy, she will serve from the heart, stepping out of her ego, meeting her reader on the road, right where she is, not telling her she should be or go anywhere else.

When you serve, you drop the judgment, the stories, the righteousness. You embrace your reader for who they are, where they are. And you love them, fiercely, with every single word you type.

Do you want change for them? OH, HELL YEAH – with all your bleeding heart. But you know, you are an author that makes a difference, not an author that pushes people around.

THE DIFFERENCE PROCESS
STEP 1 – DEFINE YOUR IDEAL READER

You've probably heard me say this before, but the most common misstep first time authors make is that they start their book by writing it. If you aren't convinced this time, head on over to www.TheAuthorIncubator.com and sign up for the free four-part video series which goes with this book. Those four classes will explain in more detail why that is a problem, so I don't want you to miss it.

But if you aren't going to start your book by writing, what the heck are you going to be doing with your time?

One you have the problem you can solve in hand, focus exclusively on getting to know how your ideal reader would describe the problem.

Let's say you have mastered the art of mindfulness, and you can help people who are arguing with reality to relax. Okay! That's a great skill and a great start. But now, you need to think like Sandra with her dating book. Very few people want mindfulness, or to stop arguing with reality. They want their boss to treat them properly, or their tinnitus to go away. In fact, let's take tinnitus as an example.

Author, blogger and all-round genius Jonathan Fields wrote in his 2011 Annual Report, which you can find right over here (http://jonathanfields.wpengine.netdna-cdn.com/blog/wp-content/uploads/2012/01/Annual-Report-2011.pdf) that he was suffering from tinnitus, a mysterious and neurologically intense condition that causes loud ringing noises in the ear and extreme stress. Here's Jonathan:

> *Mainstream medicine offers no cure, only masks that work in varying degrees. A battery of scans and an endless stream of tests ruled out much of the big scary stuff, but left me an emotional wreck, largely unable to sleep or focus for months. ....*
> *I've explored nearly every mainstream and complimentary therapy available....*
> *For me, mindfulness, work-flow adaptations, environmental optimization,*

positive psychology and movement aren't just about peak performance, they are about being okay in my world. They're the foundation of my ability to deal with not only the ever-present noise in my head, but a variety of evolving physiological learning opportunities, and the possibility that any or all might change or become amplified on any given day. They've even opened me to the challenge of embracing a source of potential torment as my teacher. ...It's inspired me to go a lot deeper into what it means to live a good life with the time I have, in whatever state greets me.

So Mr. Fields has found that mindfulness helped him address his tinnitus, and makes it more manageable. But he also found that he could, as he says, "embrace a source of potential torment as my teacher."

He could be called to write a book called *Torment by Tinnitus: Why I Love It!* Heck, who knows, there might be someone who responds really well to that. But if his ideal reader is someone like him – a successful business person and creator who is suddenly paralyzed by inescapable and discordant noise inside his own head, is that really the message that's going to resonate? (Pun intended.)

No, if the ideal reader was Jonathan Fields when the tinnitus first kicked off, he has already told us, he first went to the doctor and looked for traditional medicine or diagnosis. So that wouldn't have been the time to grab him with a book about mindfulness. But when all the traditional roads were turning into dead ends, he looked for "complementary therapy" – that's our first keyword clue. He wasn't looking for mindfulness instruction, necessarily – that would have sounded weird and scary and irrelevant. Even though your book *could* have made a difference to him, it never would have.

To make a difference. you would have had to call your book something like *STOP THE NOISE: Complementary Therapies for Tinnitus Sufferers.* And yes, inside you get to teach everything you want about mindfulness. But first, you have to serve.

So let's create an Ideal Reader Profile, to help you get to know your reader right at the moment before they search on Amazon and find your book – which is, again, their ticket out of hell. Answer these questions for your One Perfect Reader that this entire book can be a big, juicy love letter to. Yes, other people will read the book, but for now don't worry about those people. Let's build a profile of "The One."

- What their gender? (Any issues with that?)
- How old are they, and how do they feel about their age?
- Do they have a partner? If so, how is that relationship?
- Where do they live? How do they feel about their City or Town?
- Kids? Do they have, or wish they had kids? How's their relationship with them if they've got 'em?
- What kind of work do they do? What is their mindset around their job?
- How is their general health? Any medical issues in their life?
- What's their relationship with their parents like?
- What are they most worried about?

- What keeps them up at night or wakes them up at night?
- What are they searching for on Google to address the problem?
- If your ideal reader could snap their fingers and change one thing in their life instantly, what would it be? (Make sure this is in their words – not if you could snap your fingers for them.)
- If they don't buy your book, how will they solve this problem?

One your profile is complete, and you feel like, if cast, you could play your ideal reader in the biopic of their life, then it's time to "get into character as your ideal reader" and pick one or more of these three challenges:

1. **Visual Challenge**: Create a vision board for your ideal reader from their perspective. Get into their head – what do they want and desire more of in their life? What would they clip out of a magazine?

2. **Aural Challenge**: Create a playlist of songs this reader is listening to for comfort and support as they are struggling with this problem.

3. **Written Challenge**: Write a letter from your ideal reader to his or her best friend. Better yet, if you are a text messaging sort of person, write a chat style conversation between them!

When you know your ideal reader that well, you are ready to move on to the next step.

Inside the Author Incubator:
On Being Ready

Q: What if I'm not "fixed" yet? I haven't totally figured this out for myself, how can I write about it?

A: I've had so many authors-in-transformation ask me this question, but one story sticks in my head. We had an amazingly heart-centered conversation about her book, which was the story of surviving beyond the suicide of an adult child. Her son had taken his life several years before, and she had been working with parents fresh from grief with a child who had much more recently taken their own life.

When she said this to me, I was aware of the dozens of parents who had lost a child who she had helped with her story and her ability to hold the space for such a massive emotional load. She said: "But I am not over his death and I miss him every day and some days I still think about taking my life so I don't have to live with this crushing pain. How can I possibly help other people when I haven't fixed this yet?"

I have a shocking announcement. Whether it's something as tragic and weighty as a child's suicide or something as trivial as nail biting, you are probably never going to be "fixed." You'll never have it totally figured out. That's sort of the point of being alive. And more importantly, it's the wrong way to frame the challenge – in life or in writing a book that makes a difference.

When you understand your ideal reader, and what their awareness of their problem is, you can start to see that you don't need to have everything figured out, just enough to get them to the next leg of their journey.

I look at it this way. For a long time, I was 100 pounds or more overweight. When I would see a perfect-looking skinny blonde giving weight loss advice, I'd almost never listen. I liked my weight loss advice coming from folks with a little more meat on their bones. If they were 200 lbs. now and they had been 400 lbs. That was the kind of weight loss guru I needed.

To help the people you were born to help, you only need to be one leap ahead of them, not a whole country mile.

Have a question for The Author Incubator? Send me your ideas, comments and complaints. I want to know what you think. You can reach me at:

TheAuthorIncubator.com/contact-us

CHAPTER TWO:
WHO ARE YOU?
I REALLY WANNA KNOW.

For one person to be able to advise, or even help another, a lot must happen, a lot must go well, a whole constellation of things must come right in order once to succeed.

~ Rainer Maria Rilke, Letters to a Young Poet

Once you know who your reader is, your book can become a love letter from them, to you. But in order to write the love letter, we need to know who *you* are in this two-way love affair.

The quote above is from my favorite poet, Rainer Maria Rilke. From 1902 to 1908, Rilke, by then a published and successful poet, engaged in a six-year friendship and mentorship with novice poet Franz Xaver Kappus. In the eighth letter published in *Letters to a Young Poet*, Rilke said to his protégé of the experience:

"Do not believe that he who seeks to comfort you lives untroubled among the simple and quiet words that sometimes do you good. His life has much difficulty and sadness. ... Were it otherwise, he would never have been able to find those words."

In my opinion this book is the best personal growth book written in all of human history. I know bible scholars are going to argue with me here, but in this tiny volume I have found echoes of every major life lesson I've ever faced. And what I think makes this book so incredibly powerful is that Rilke wasn't trying to change the world, he was trying to make a difference to one young man. The intimacy of this book is at the heart of its depth and power.

That's the kind of depth and power I want for you for your book. But to do that, you need to know who you are.

When Rilke wrote to Kappus, he knew they were "brothers" of a sort, since they both graduated from the same school. Rilke was 8 years senior to Kappus, and had published 5 volumes of poetry that had been well received, prior to Kappus contacting him.

Kappus made Rilke's job as an author mentor easier because he came to him with the specific problem: Should I become a poet, or play it safe and go for a career in the military like my dad? But Kappus was tricky in that he didn't ask the question that way. What he said was: "Are my poems good enough for me to ditch the safe path, and go for it as a poet?"

If Rilke were my author, and Kappus his "ideal reader," I might have suggested Rilke call his book something like: *Just Good or Truly Great: How to Know When Your Poetry is so Fantastic You'd be a Fool to do Anything Else but Pursue it As a Career.* Now, inside that book, Rilke would change nothing from *Letters to a Young Poet.* Rilke never answers Kappus' question. Because, of course, it's the wrong question – just like Sandra's question about how to tell if a guy is honest in the previous example. Instead, Rilke explains how a poet would make that decision, by advising him on how a poet should feel, love, seek truth, and make meaning about his art and the world.

His role is part guru or sage. His voice has an almost mystical quality and the confidence that comes with not feeling beholden to answering Kappus' actual question.

He is, most clearly, taking on the voice of a mentor – more formal than a big brother, more intimate than a guru. Rilke is the mentor, Kappus is the protégé, and thus a relationship is born. It is the relationship that we must establish in order for you to write your love letter.

Let's say Kappus was your ideal reader – a young artist deciding between a safe, but boring, job and a riskier path that is true to his heart. Who would you be to that reader? I'm going to go out on a limb here, and guess you didn't go to school with Kappus and you don't have five volumes of published poetry and a budding career as a member of the literati. So the role of mentor isn't looking good for you. So who could you be?

A parent-figure perhaps?

A teacher?

A comrade-in-arms?

Can you see how if you don't make this determination, you literally *cannot* write a love letter? The love letter can't be to a young poet from his mom, teacher, or a friend. That's not a love letter, that's an instruction manual for putting together a bookcase.

You and your reader are two halves of a whole for this process, twin flames. One cannot burn brightly without the other. So to be in service, you must decide who you are, and stick with that decision.

Google "world's best love letters," or some search terms like that. You will find there are love letters from many different lovers: a husband to his wife; a gay man married to a woman writing to his young male muse; a husband to his pregnant wife written as if it were penned by their dog; a King to his mistress. But there is no "best" love letter from an unspecified sender.

The Author's Identity Crisis

So who are you in relation to your reader? This is the question on the table, and it's a question only you can answer.

One of my authors was fascinated by neuroscience, and wanted to know if there was a connection between what brain scientists were finding out about how the neural pathways work and the vague theories that drive the Law of Attraction. She knew her ideal reader was a Law of Attraction skeptic. But as a Law of Attraction fan, who was *she*? She could be someone trying to convince the skeptic they were wrong, but that's not really a love letter is it? Maybe a passive aggressive love letter, but not what we were going for.

She could be a coach, showing them how they could apply this knowledge to reach their own goals. But if they were already ready to set goals based on the knowledge, then she was changing the ideal reader. Then they weren't really a skeptic at all. They were a fan who wanted more technical information on how it works. Fine, but that's a different book.

She thought about being a teacher, but when she tried that on, it felt heavy – like a burden. She wasn't an expert yet, she was just investigating this. What if she was wrong? Claiming the role of neuroscience expert seemed a bit much. And that's when it hit her. She could be an investigative journalist. You, dear reader, are a skeptic – and so am I. If there is any hard science to this Law of Attraction stuff, I'm going to use my shoe leather and find it! It's you and I, together, on a mission to discover: The Truth.

BINGO!

Now we have the makings for a love letter. Sender and receiver defined.

THE DIFFERENCE PROCESS
STEP 2 – IDENTIFY YOUR VOICE

It's your turn now. Here's what I want you to do. And even if you THINK you know what your relationship is to your ideal reader, do this anyway because you might make some subtle shifts that take your relationship to the next level.

First, you have to have the problem clearly defined – in one sentence, with no commas. This must be a sentence your love would actually say. If it's a little embarrassingly vulnerable, all the better!

Here are some examples:

- I want my boyfriend to treat me like a princess instead of an afterthought.
- I only want to lose weight if I know I can keep it off permanently this time.

- I want to get over my fear of driving on the highway, which I know is stupid.

Then pull out your ideal reader description, and write a one-sentence reply to the problem in each of five different characters. Pick from this list or write some alternatives of your own:

- Investigative reporter
- New Yorker magazine style journalist
- Ira Glass style story teller
- Their mother
- A loving, but off-the-beaten-path aunt
- A CEO with a company that has a product that solves this problem
- A life coach
- A spiritual guru
- A ding-bat neighbor
- Their best friend
- A lover
- An industry expert
- The enemy
- A serious professional like a doctor, lawyer, or therapist
- An academic or scientific researcher

- A kid
- A sibling
- A comedian who does actually get it

You can even try writing the sentence without clarifying your relationship. Just "be yourself" and see how it comes out.

Here, let me show you.

Problem: I've wanted to write a book for 30+ years and no matter how many times I start, I never finish.

Investigative reporter persona: Let's go inside the minds of the world's most prolific writers. What is it that makes it so easy for them to produce book after book, while others struggle alone with their mission?

Ira Glass Style story teller: A strange thing happens when you start to write a book. You see, I always thought writing was easy, it was finishing that was hard. And then I met Starleigh Kane, and I figured out I'd had it all backwards.

Life Coach: For many people, writing a book is a goal they have set but failed to achieve. They might think the problem is outside of themselves, but the truth is the only thing stopping you from achieving this goal is your thoughts. So let's start there: what do you make it mean that you haven't written your book yet?

Lover: My love, My heart, My dear one. Do you not know how your words sing to the world when you share them? I want to catch your words as they are falling off your lips and kiss each one.

An Industry Expert: So, you want to write a book! That's great! There are a few simple things you need to know to get started in a way that makes you most likely to finish. First....

You get the idea. Try on as many personas as you can until you find one that fits and feels natural. Note the last one, the industry expert, sounds quite a bit like me. I've modified the typical Industry Expert to an industry expert who is heart-centered and service-oriented. But essentially, that's me.

When you try on a bunch of these personas, you can see how different the same book with the same problem and the same solution can be. And you'll also see how weird and mushy your writing is when you have a love letter with a 'To' address and no one specific on the 'From' line.

Inside the Author Incubator:
On the Fraud Factor

Q: What if I'm actually just a big phony, and I have no business writing a book?

A: Questions like this always have something to do with the fraud factor – a fear of getting found out, when the book comes out, that they just aren't very good.

I love this comment from actress and singer Michelle Pfeiffer: "I still think people will find out that I'm really not very talented. I'm not very good. It's all been a big sham."

Let's start here. Everyone has doubts. I can set my watch by them. I know exactly *when* in the writing and publishing process my authors will call me to say they think they should drop out because it's not going to be very good. And here's what I tell them:

Doubts can be good; they can inspire you to become better. In fact, I'd be more worried if you didn't have doubts. I even find women who have easy pregnancies suspicious. You are making a person. Shouldn't it be just a little hard and scary? (This from the woman who threw up every single day of her 41-week pregnancy!)

Feeling like a fraud can actually make you work harder and write an even better book. What we don't want doubt to do is paralyze you.

My mentor explained it to me this way: there is an area of your life where you aren't very good at being a full adult. So, you have hired me to fill in that gap. I'll make sure you'll do what you said you wanted to do, even when you get scared and want to change your mind.

That's the role I play for my clients struggling with Imposter Syndrome pre-publication. I get to be the adult for them and keep them moving forward, even though it's scary. Impostor Syndrome is incredibly common, and no matter how smart, accomplished, or creative – a lot of us have these thoughts at some point. There's no reason to let that derail your dream.

If you don't have a book coach, a publisher, or an editor who can play that role for you, you'll want to play around with the idea that you have accomplished a lot of things in your life and some of them have required pushing through this obstacle. Try to find one goal you have achieved where you felt like a fraud at first but proceeded, and succeeded, anyway. Can you identify the thought you were thinking that made it possible to overcome the fear?

Let's say you had to speak in public on a topic you weren't ideally confident about. You felt like the audience might doubt your credibility on the topic, but you did it anyway. What was the thought? *I'll get fired if I don't do this.* Or, *It's only going to be 5 minutes, then it will be over. Maybe it won't be as bad as I think.* Once you find the thought that shoved Impostor Syndrome aside, see if you can create something similar and truer for this situation.

This is a reverse version of Brooke Castillo's Self-Coaching 101 method. So if you are stuck on this step, get a copy of her book at Amazon, and see if you can work the model. Or set up a call with me, and I'll work you through it.

To set up a call with me, just email Info@TheAuthorIncubator.com and someone on my team will hook you up with access to my calendar.

Have a question for The Author Incubator? Send me your ideas, comments and complaints. I want to know what you think. You can reach me at:

TheAuthorIncubator.com/contact-us

CHAPTER THREE:
WHAT DO YOU
REALLY WANT?

Begin with the end in mind.
~ Stephen Covey, 7 Habits of Highly Effective People

Alright love! I have some good news. If you have reached this chapter having done the work to identify the problem, e.g. you are going to solve and to figure out the protagonists for your love letter, you have done much of the heavy lifting in the saga known as writing a book that matters. Now we can move on to talking about your favorite topic: *you!*

One of the ways procrastination and writer's block weasel their ways into writer's lives is that the author doesn't have clarity of purpose. If your Inner Author feels like this whole book thing is going to turn out to be a big waste of time, she'll protect you by making it virtually impossible to write.

For years, I have hosted a podcast called "Book Journeys." All of our guests have finished and published their books. I ask each guest about writer's block, and very few of them have much to say on the matter. You know why? Because they finished!

Writer's block is for people who want to *want* to write a book. There are a lot of book coaches out there who help people more effectively *want* to have a book. Most writer's workshops or online writing classes are the same. They cater to your wants and your *wanting*. You may improve your writing skills, but in most cases you won't end up an author. The program is not created to support your growth in that way.

When I created my YOUR DELICIOUS BOOK program, I only wanted to attract authors-in-transformation. Not worms who were happily munching on apples – but caterpillars who would absolutely, positively become butterflies. We didn't build a program that would keep people stuck in wanting, or eternally locked in cycles of developing ideas. We built a program that guarantees you will move forward. You don't have a to-do list at the end of this program, you have an actual, finished book.

But the secret is – this program is only for people who are ready to *claim* their status as an author. The people who are attracted to working with me don't simply *want* to write a book. They are doing it.

I know all too well how subtle this distinction is, because I lived in this gap of wanting for the sake of want for most of my life. I think I've already mentioned that I used to be 100 pounds overweight. Well, there is a little more to the story. I also lost 100 pounds. Not once. Not twice. But five times. FIVE!!!! And do you know why I did this five times? I really liked having this *problem* lurking over me. It was comfortable, and I was good at *wanting* to lose weight.

I was *miserable* on so many levels, and yet, I was really fucking content with having an extra 100 pounds of fat on my body because it made it so easy for me to keep my dreams small. It virtually eliminated all pressure to do anything (except lose the weight). It gave me a reason for every failure or bad experience. I didn't have to feel most of my feelings. I could just focus on hating my fat. If I wasn't getting what I wanted out of life, I had the perfect excuse at my finger tips. "I NEED TO LOSE WEIGHT…. And then I can worry about grad school, a promotion, getting a boyfriend, planning a trip, buying a house, having a baby, etc)."

When I lost weight, I lost that delightful excuse. I couldn't hide behind my fat anymore. I had to act on my desires, not put them in a queue behind my diet.

For many of my clients, the perpetual excuse is: "I'm working on my book." Or, "Once I write my book, then I'll _____. " In actuality, this act of waiting and wanting is really a creative way of lying to ourselves.

So ask yourself:

What do you want?

What are you content with having?

How big are you willing to let yourself dream?

Maybe you want a successful business, or you want to write a book, or you want a partner who gets you at every level. But if you are content living without it – *if you are living without it right now* – you won't make those dreams come true. You have to get uncomfortable enough to take action.

A lot of times, we think misery and beating ourselves up about something counts as action. It doesn't. Whether it's our weight problem, our inability to focus, not feeling good enough or qualified enough – being miserable about it is a sign we actually are content with what we have. And we've even given it a place in our life to stay. You know when I lost weight for good? When I *stopped* being miserable about it, and just did it. I was done. I gave up the comfort and contentment of having a permanent excuse for being less than what I was born to be.

Ask yourself if there are ways you are *content* with not having a book. Does *wanting* to write a book give you any excuses or a good story to tell? Is there a way *not* having a book is actually serving you?

Here's what I have found for myself: once you really decide you are *done* – done being fat, done playing small, done saying you *want* to write a book, done *wanting* anything – then you just go get it. Full stop. When you are ready, you will just do it. No more questions. No more waiting. No more *wanting*. It's like it's already done in the world, and you just need to connect the dots between here and there.

The authors-in-transformation who sign up for my YOUR DELICIOUS BOOK program have decided they have already written a book that is going to transform their business and make a difference in the lives of their readers. Then they just have to connect the dots. When they are this ready, our program makes it a guarantee that will happen. That's why they pick our program. The trick is in pulling the trigger.

If you don't want a book, you'll sign up for a writing workshop or you'll join a writer's circle. These are programs that can LOOK like forward action, but don't have a path forward or a clear intention, and these are blocks that keep you stuck in a holding pattern of wanting.

THE DIFFERENCE PROCESS
STEP 3 – FRAME YOUR OUTCOME

Now, if you *do* want to write a book, you need to answer this question. What's the point?

Writing a book is a challenge, not unlike climbing a mountain or running a marathon. It takes preparation, supplies and support, and you can do it. But first, you have to know *why*. There are lots of reasons to write a book. Here are some common reasons I hear from authors:

- To change someone's life.
- To share my passion for something I know a lot about.
- To make money.
- To get the book that's inside me out of me.
- To be creative.
- To write down everything I know.
- To increase my credibility.

- To become a world-famous "Go-To" Expert.
- To gain a competitive edge.
- To create a passive income stream.
- To move into areas such as training, consulting, and presenting.
- To have a platform from which to network with new people/a new industry.
- To learn new skills, or expand the ones you already hold.
- To leave a legacy of your work.
- To make your mom/spouse/kid(s) proud.

Any of these ringing a bell? Can you rank them?

Think about how you'll feel when you have reached that goal. How will your life be different? Will you have a sense of purpose? More clients? Clarity about your future?

Once you've got that feeling identified, I like to go to the next steps and really specifically frame your outcome. How is your life going to be different 12 months after your book gets published?

In most cases, even if you write a book that matches your goal, there is still work to do right now. Books, ladies and gentlemen, do not sell, advertise, or promote themselves.

Let's take the goals of creating passive income from your book and just making money from your book in general.

Did you only want to make money from book sales? Most books sell fewer than 1,000 copies. Even if you self-publish, 1,000 copies is not going to pay for your trip to the Bahamas, much less your retirement. How will you create a plan that leads to actual book sales? One test you can run is to try to pre-sell 100 books using Pubslush, Indiegogo, or another crowdfunding platform. If you can't pre-sell 100 books on your topic, you aren't going to sell 100,000 after your book is released.

The best way to make money from a non-fiction book – and it's the best way to help people, too – is to tie your book to a paid speaking, coaching or consulting offer. Maybe all three! Develop a plan for what you are going to create alongside your book while you are writing your book, and presell it. Again, if you can't get 10 people to buy a $100 class on the same topic as your book, you are going to have a hard time getting 10,000 people to buy your book.

In the Your Delicious Book program, we calculate your revenue goal for the book, including the book as only one of the streams of income. We identify how many coaching clients, speaking gigs, and consulting opportunities you need to derive from your book to hit that revenue goal. Then we make sure you write a book that is going to make the likelihood of your reaching those goals pretty high.

Can you come up with a similar plan? If it seems overwhelming, I'm happy to help. Reach out to me for a private strategy session to map the outcome of your book at info@TheAuthorIncubator.com.

Inside the Author Incubator:
On Money

Q: How much money can I make from my book?

A: After helping hundreds of coaches and entrepreneurs finish and make a difference with their books, I know what a huge commitment writing a book is for you. It's not only the investment you make financially, and with your blood sweat and tears in writing the book – it's been a years-long, or even a decades-long commitment to get the message into people's hearts. That's no easy or quiet feat. So it makes sense to want to know what you are going to get in return.

I have had clients earning six figures from coaching and consulting that came directly from their books, within mere months after the release. I've cheered for authors who filled workshops with dozens, even hundreds of clients, just weeks after publishing their book. I've seen authors who have never spoken for money before, confidently taking in mid- to high-five-figure speaking opportunities within days of publishing. And, I've watched the impact of an author's work being featured on major national websites within hours of the release. Becoming an author will change your life, and more importantly, it will make a difference to the thousands or even millions of people you have knowledge and insights to help.

So, the only question left is about you – are you willing to stand up and share your gifts with the people whose lives you were born to change, or are you going to be stingy?

Have a question for The Author Incubator? Send me your ideas, comments and complaints. I want to know what you think. You can reach me at:

TheAuthorIncubator.com/contact-us

CHAPTER FOUR:
MAKING TIME OUT OF
NOTHING AT ALL

EINSTEIN TIME gives you a way to expand the amount of time you need for creative expression and intimate connections.

~ Gay Hendricks, Einstein Time

Way back when I was an overweight, unhappy, corporate drone, I made a decision to find the thing I loved most in the world and turn that into a career. I searched for 3 years for my "thing." What did I lose track of time doing?

Here is the list I came up with:

1. Talking to Jenny about anything
2. Playing cribbage or Rummy 500
3. Surfing the Internet

None of these things looked like the path to personal and financial freedom. I read every personal growth book on the market to try to figure this out. I went to workshops. I took personality tests. I tried everything to get to my "bliss."

And then, one day, as I was driving home from work, it hit me! I have over 5,000 self-help books! *That's* my thing! I want to spend every minute of my working life creating the type of books I love! And in that moment, a business was born.

The best thing about my job, is that all day long, I read the kinds of books that change my life. One of my early clients was an amazing life coach named Jill Farmer. I was working with Jill on her book *There's Not Enough Time... and other lies we tell ourselves*, when I figured out the secret to getting a book done.

Most of my clients, up to that point, said they loved working with me and got a lot out of our sessions, but Jill was the only one who had actually finished her book. Why? Because she had the missing piece to the productivity puzzle. Here's Jill:

The culprit for my out of control ride was all in my head. The never-ending time shortage story I kept telling myself launched a vortex that sucked me in, leaving me dizzy, disoriented and desperate for a time fix. Until I put the brakes on a very old pattern of thinking, no efficiency program or time management system I had adopted would make things better. The source of my woes was well-hidden in my subconscious.

That's *right*! The reason you think you don't have time to write your book is because you *think* you don't have time to write your book, if only subconsciously. I know it may sound syllogistic, but in this case, it's true.

As Gay Hendricks, author of *The Big Leap* explains, "When you make the shift to Einstein Time, you experience a major surge in your productivity, creativity and enjoyment." When it comes to writing a book, what Hendricks calls Einstein Time, I call, "Focusing Your Author Mojo."

Your Inner Author WANTS to write. Always. *You* are the problem. And the good news is, *you* are also the solution. In fact, these mere thoughts will interfere with your forward progress: "I don't have enough time to write my book," or, "I wish I had more time for my book." We think that declaring our desire is enough.

So Step 1 in Focusing Your Author Mojo is dropping that big lie.

How do I know it's a lie? I mean, come on, I don't even KNOW you. You could be a neuroscientist with 27 kids and 4 wives. Maybe you really don't have time. Nope again! Those are merely circumstances. Circumstances cannot keep your Inner Author down. Only thoughts and beliefs have the power to do that.

I've got a video on this in my free four-part video series. If you haven't signed up for it yet, head on over to www.TheAuthorIncubator.com and sign in right next to the video of me to watch.

The first thing you have to understand about finding time to write a book is this: You do have enough time. People with more work, family, and health issues than you have gotten it done. CEOs, political candidates, and music moguls are busier than you, and they have written books.

I mean when Barack Obama wrote his bestseller *The Audacity of Hope*, he was a US Senator with a working wife, two little kids, and a presidential campaign to run. Did he have help, sure, but you can choose to have help, too!

Finding time to write a book is a choice he made. It's a choice you can make, too, but it starts with your thoughts.

In order for your Author Mojo to work for you, you have to get really clear on why you are writing the book. If you don't start with a clear outcome in mind, your brain will find ways to fill time without getting your book done. This is actually your Inner Author's way of protecting you from wasting time on something that won't work. It's a good thing, and it's why we've already done the "Frame your Outcome" step.

The second thing to remember about finding time is this: the authors I've worked with who have the best results have one thing in common; they made a clear decision that they would finish. It sounds simple, but it's a major step. My clients sign a contract, make a commitment to me and my team, and they make a financial investment which you'd only be willing to make if you were totally committed to finishing. Most importantly, they know the exact date (no if, ands, or buts) that their book will be in their hands – and they prepare themselves for its arrival, much like expectant parents would upon hearing the due date for their first child.

The third key to finding time and finishing your book is in changing your thoughts about yourself when you aren't writing. You know, your subtle self-talk. It's hard to believe, but thinking of yourself as a procrastinator, or feeling like you aren't getting enough done on your book fast enough can create a shame cycle that slows your book progress down to a crawl. My clients know the simple fix to this problem is relabeling you activities when you feel like you are procrastinating. When you identify them as a way of working on your book, and get honest about what's really going on, procrastination and writer's block float in and out but shorten their stays, because there isn't anything for them to stick to.

Cleaning Out My Closet

Take my client, Jenn, for example. When she was working on her book, she found that little things in her house started to bother her. She'd sit down to write, and be plagued with a burning desire to organize her kids' toys. (Don't judge. I promise she's very nice.)

So her calendar would be telling her: "It's time to write!" But her heart and soul was begging for toy organization time. Off she'd go, into the time-space vortex of cleaning every corner of the playroom, and another day's writing time would evaporate into the ether.

What did we do to focus her Author Mojo?

We relabeled organizing toys as working on her book. I know, I know this can sound like a lie, but see if you can follow the rationale:

When Jenn sat down to write, but instead had the urge to organize, she'd begin to beat herself up for not being focused, or not being committed enough to her work. She'd get mad at herself and the entire time she'd be cleaning up toys, she'd be self-flagellating her Inner Author for being bad.

Why didn't her Inner Author show up on time to the party? Why wasn't she overcome with a burning desire to write her book at the correct time and place?

Well, I don't know about you, but if someone yells at me for not showing up to their party on time, it does *not* make me want to come earlier next time. Being yelled at does not make me want to play. It makes me want to run and hide. That's what her Inner Author was doing. The more Jenn beat herself up, the less she'd write.

When we Focused her Author Mojo, we were able to reframe the toy organization urge into a cute little Inner Author quirk. "Okay babe," she'd say to her Inner Author, "you don't want to write right now. Cool. Let's go clean the kids' playroom and see how you feel in 15 minutes." She'd set a timer, and check in. If her Inner Author wanted to write in 15 minutes, she'd be ready and waiting. If not, more toy organization, no self-abuse. Just curiosity.

"It's totally cool if we do this today, but I'm just wondering why you don't want to write."

With love and self-care, Jenn was able to identify the real obstacle to writing and get back to it. Her total word count was so much higher as a result than if she beat herself into submission (or what I call white-knuckling it), and so even with the reduced time in her writing schedule, she got more done.

You know how I said "toy organization" was working on her book?

Here's why.

If there is a one-hour writing window you have set aside, and you don't feel like writing, you have a couple of clear options. You can force yourself into writing, and you will get some work done – but it's probably not going to be your best work, and it's probably not going to be very usable. Based on experience, I'm guessing you'd end up with a usable word count of 500 words and a complimentary neck ache.

Option two, if you don't feel like writing, is to take that hour, clean up the playroom, and beat yourself up. Total word count seems like it would be zero, but you have also done psychic damage to your Inner Author – so showing up to write next time is going to be even harder. Let's say you end up with a total word count of - 250 words. And a migraine.

When you choose option 3 and Focus Your Author Mojo, something magical happens. The first 15 minutes, total words – zero. Maybe after 15 minutes, your Inner Author is still feeling shy, that's cool. But at 30 minutes in, you feel the urge to write. When you sit down, you'll notice the words pour from your soul. You can barely type fast enough to keep up with your thoughts, and each sentence is more gorgeously crafted than the last. You look up – and see that an hour has gone by. You're late for your next appointment, but somehow you have 2,500 fantastic words. Best of all, you can't wait to sit down and write again.

And, so you can see, cleaning the toys (from a place of joy and with the mindset of doing it as a way to work on her book), was the absolute best way to work on Jenn's book.

THE DIFFERENCE PROCESS
STEP 4 – FOCUS YOUR AUTHOR MOJO

Creating a writing ritual

One of the ways to "trick" the brain into writing mode is to have a small ritual you perform before you start writing. This can be as small as putting on a hat that says, "Author At Work," or ringing a bell. Design a small ritual you can create that would be easy to execute from where you imagine doing most of your writing. For me, it's brewing a cup of Yorkshire Tea in my Free Your Inner Author mug.

In fact, here's a fun idea! If you want to make that your ritual, I'll send you a Free Your Inner Author mug. You will love it.

All you have to do is email your desire to info@TheAuthorIncubator.com. We'll schedule a call to talk about your book, and at the end of that call, remind me about the mug – and I'll put one in the mail to you, absolutely free.

How Your Inner Author Wants It

Next, here's what I want you to do. For one week, write every day. You can write things you know will go in your book, or just google the phrase "writing prompts," and pick some every day, even if that means you write on a random topic.

Make notes about the following:

1. How long does it would take you to write 500 words about a topic you were comfortable with? You may want to do a timed test – for instance, you can write a 500 word description of your house and time it – to validate your optimal writing speed.

2. What time of day have you been most successful in writing?

3. When you write, or work on a project, about how long do you like to sit and work for? Just fifteen minutes? Four

whole hours? What feels good to you? Do you recharge at intervals and go back to it? What are those?

4. How do you like to be dressed when you write? (Guilty confession, I write in long stretches and do not like to change outfits until I finish – the whole book. When I wrote my dissertation, which was over 50,000 words, I barely left the house. In fact, I wore the same pink striped pajama pants for days and days and days on end. I don't know... my Inner Author liked them. A lot.)

We want to find your Inner Author's happy place. So once we know these things, we can schedule you writing time with the right conditions to make your Inner Author most likely to want to come out and play. Then, if you find yourself unwilling to or uninteresting in writing one day, remember Jenn's story. Focusing your Author Mojo means always treating your Inner Author with respect and love. We'll talk about this more in chapter 8, but for now, just figure out what your Inner Author's optimal writing conditions are.

There is always enough time to write your book. Resistance, however, does not play by the rules of Einstein Time. To free yourself from the Newtonian time space continuum and get this book written, learning how to Focus Your Author Mojo is key.

INSIDE THE AUTHOR INCUBATOR:
ON LIMITATIONS

Q: What if I have a medical condition that makes writing, typing or even sitting for long stretches difficult? Does that mean I can't write a book?

A: You can totally write a book even if you can't type or sit for a long time. Here's what I recommend. Follow the steps in this book until you get to the writing part. Instead of writing each chapter, plan to speak each chapter into an audio recorder.

You'll want to record between one and two hours per chapter. I recommend turning your bullet points for each chapter into questions, and then just respond to each question. I like to make up about 10 questions to answer per chapter, and I find this gets me 10-15 pages, typed.

Bestselling author Brian Tracy, who's had more than 50 books published in 38 languages, says: "Dictating your book is one of the most powerful exercises I have ever discovered, and dramatically increases the speed at which you create your initial manuscript."

Once the recordings are done, send the files off to a transcriptionist. At The Author Incubator, we use a service called YakWrite, but simply Google "audio transcription," and you'll find a plethora of options, most charging between $1 and $5 per audio minute. Transcription in hand, you now have a first draft of your manuscript. Send it to a fantastic editor to polish it up, and *voila*! Authorhood awaits!

Have a question for The Author Incubator? Send me your ideas, comments and complaints. I want to know what you think. You can reach me at:

www.TheAuthorIncubator.com/contact-us

CHAPTER FIVE:
I BELIEVE I CAN FLY

Our brains cannot tell the difference between an external, "real" thing and an imagined version of it.
~ Janette Dalgliesh, Mastering Your Everyday Superpower

I'm not here to tell you the way to get your book done is to put it on your vision board and wait for a muse or a fairy to drop by with a finished book ready and waiting for you. I believe in magic and all, but at the end of the day, I'm pretty brass-tacks.

I will tell you, however, that there is no way you can write the book you were born to write if you don't envision your success. I always thought of this as my "Law of Attraction" step, and then I met an amazing woman, Janette Dalgliesh, who also happens to be an author we publish here at Difference Press. Janette helped my inner scientist understand exactly why this step is so crucial.

Before I explain it though, I need to tell you a story.

When you write the book you were born to write, you can choose to write it from a place of joy and ease. All those horror stories about writing can be someone else's business, and maybe it was their personal truth. I didn't know this when I wrote my first book. My first book is called *Medea to Media: Live Performance as a Vehicle for Social Change*. It was originally written as my Ph.D. dissertation, when I was finishing my PhD in a gorgeous town in the Swiss Alps called Saas Fee.

The topic was something very close to my heart. I was exploring the connection between theatre and other live performances, and the progressive advances a community makes socially and politically, as codified in law. This was an undertaking that required rigorous content analysis as well as the synthesis and interpretation of some of the world's most dense, complex and challenging philosophy – as written by names such as Gadamer, Wittgenstein, and Derrida.

Now don't worry if you don't know anything about philosophy and cannot relate to my predicament. Just know this – it was NOT an easy paper to write. To make matters worse, one of the members of my dissertation committee had a vested interest in not giving me a passing grade. My book specifically attacked recorded music and films – and the rise and popularity of recorded performance – for slower progress on social issues. In other words, I was kind of saying, movies were bad. The committee member with the vested interest? Renowned and revolutionary filmmaker, John Waters!

I knew the other two members of my committee – playwright and cultural studies scholar Kerric Harvey and my advisor Wolfgang Schumacher – would support my theories, and I knew what kinds of questions they would ask. But I expected John Waters to be the loose cannon.

I was his TA for a class called *FILTH,* and we worked together well. Some days, after class, we'd smoke Marlboro Reds together by the ping-pong tables on our campus and shoot the shit about the differences between DC and Baltimore. John is the nicest, most incredibly normal, really, really smart guy you'd ever want to meet. And I really wanted him on my committee – until I started thinking about it.

Was I calling John Waters to an academic building in Switzerland so I could tell him his movies were dumb and he should have been doing plays? I mean, what was I saying? This guy is one of the geniuses of our era, and has created more positive social change than probably any other filmmaker. I was mortified to have asked him. But then, how do you un-invite John Waters from being on your dissertation committee?

I started second guessing all my theories, and I kept imagining John Waters looking on, disappointed in me. His pencil-thin mustache and eyes pointing away in disgust. The sinking feeling of knowing he'd never share another Marlboro Red with me again.

As I started to write, I noticed this "third eye" on me. It's as though I was writing, but also watching myself write. Almost lik there was another "me" – the guardian of my nascent friendship with a hero of mine from my high school days – was making sure I didn't pull any funny business.

Writing became an exercise in torture. I bought into all the "writing is hell" drama. And I mostly practiced envisioning my book not being finished, and not being published. My "line" at the time was: *I have no evidence from my past to indicate I am capable of a task of this magnitude.*

I did finish. I turned it in. My advisor accepted it. When I got to Switzerland, I learned that John Waters had an emergency, and wouldn't be on my committee after all. This was good because I couldn't imagine facing him. But, I loved the idea of being able to grow my bond with Mr. Waters and I wanted him to read what I wrote – and at the same time, I didn't. When you think about how the Law of Attraction really works, it's no surprise something came up for him.

This all happened in the summer of 2004. And there was another surprise. Wolfgang, my advisor, had hired a new professor to oversee dissertation approval. According to the laws of the Canton Valais Ministry of Education, to get a PhD, one must publish their dissertation through an actual academic or literary publisher. Luckily, we had a university press called Atropos. All I had to do to get published was get the new guy's approval.

He didn't approve.

That's not strictly true. He approved it, conditionally, with about 100 years of rewrites. He basically threw the whole thing out. I passed my orals, with honors, but to get my Ph.D., I needed to get this thing published, and I just didn't have it in me to do the massive rewrite that was required.

I shelved it. Got married. Got pregnant. Got fat. Got fired. *I had a few things on my plate, 'k?* And then, when the dust had started to clear – five whole years later – I started to think about making those changes. But I couldn't find the manuscript.

I would fall asleep picturing the manuscript complete, and having that monster off my back. But really I was left with the to-do item called, "Find the suitcase I took to Switzerland in August 2004, and see if it's in there."

The trip to the attic seemed like a long one.

And then one day, in the summer of 2009, I got a package in the mail. It was my Ph.D. Diploma, and a letter explaining that Wolfgang had taken over approval of the written manuscripts, and my dissertation was retroactively approved for publication – without a single rewrite.

Now I understand theories of pattern matching, and if you happen to believe in coincidences, I'm sure you believe this is one. But it just seems odd to me that as soon as I *stopped* envisioning my dissertation *not* getting published, and I started envisioning it *getting* published, I was a published author with a bonus Ph.D.

So now back to my girl Janette. Janette is no stranger to the world of "woo." She knows her way around the mystical and magic, but at heart, she's a little bit more like me – a scientist. Janette and I believe in science, repeatable tests, provable theories. Things like that.

When her book *Your Everyday Superpower* came out, I was thrilled to be a part of it. Remember my dream of spending all day, everyday working on books that make the world a better place? Janette's book was definitely one of those.

What her book revealed is that neuroscientists now know, conclusively, that the brain makes "extraordinarily complex decisions based on its *best guess* at what might be going on; not an empirical, objective reality." And because of this nuance, the brain can't tell between an actual thing happening – like your dissertation being published – and your envisioning of it happening and relaxing into the idea it's a done deal. Your experience of the world isn't so much driven by what happens to you, but by how you perceive what's happening to you.

Read Janette's whole book for more on this (you can find it on amazon or through YourEverydaySuperpower.com), but what this means for you, is that if you aren't imagining your book already complete, the chance of it being completed decreases dramatically. So it's important to have a very clear picture not just of what your *book* is like when it's done, but how *you* are different when you are a published author.

THE DIFFERENCE PROCESS
STEP 5 – ENVISION YOUR SUCCESS

I like to take my authors through a guided visualization to their creativity temple where they can hop the time-space continuum, and connect with their book as already written.

If you would like me to guide you through your own visualization, so you can so a little time-space hopping, drop me a note at info@TheAuthorIncubator.com. Just put in the subject line – Creativity Temple Visualization – and we'll find a time where I can do a visualization with you or, if it's easier, send you a recording to guide you on the journey.

Beyond imaging your book complete, I want you to know exactly who you *are* once the book is published.

Imagine it's late at night, and you are alone in the house. You get a text message from an unknown number telling you there is a package on your porch (or in the mail room). You go to get the package, bring it inside and open it. Inside there is a wireless microphone and a note that reads:

> *Congratulations! You have been chosen to receive the magic microphone. You have 3 minutes to communicate to the entire world why they should read your book. Your message will be heard in the native language of every person on the planet. You've got 24 hours to use the mic, but you can only press the on button once.*

Do you know what you would say? Envison yourself with a megaphone speaking to the world with your message coming through crystal-clear to each and every soul. Call in your readers while you have the magic mic in your hand. Your book isn't for everyone, but for the people you can truly help, it will be one of the greatest blessings in their life. Envision them finding you with ease and grace. And most importantly, envision yourself being ready for the journey.

Inside the Author Incubator:
On Readiness

Q: How do I know if I'm ready?

A: Many people who tell me they want to write a book or they know they SHOULD write a book quickly follow that up with: *I'm not ready yet.*

When I talk to these prospective authors, I can tell pretty quickly if that's true or if it's an excuse. Take Sally (not her real name) –

- She told me that ever since she was a little girl she knew in her heart she was born to write a book.
- She's in her 50s now, and that message is validated and reinforced by clients and colleagues who continue to tell her she should write a book. But she says she's not ready.
- She wanted to know what I do for when she is. (First clue.)
- When I asked her when she'll be ready or how she would know she's ready, she explained she doesn't have the time or money right now to focus on it. So I asked about her business.
- She's a money coach, but she charges on a sliding scale with

clients paying between $50 and $200 per session. She doesn't want them to be afraid to spend money on a coach, so she offers a lot of pro bono work and does 20 - 40 sessions a month. (Second clue.)

- She'd like to be making $5,000 a month, but right now, she makes about half that. She has savings and some investments that she also lives off of. When she's making more, she'll write. (Third clue.)

What's wrong with this picture? Do you see it?

First, the credibility and confidence being a published author adds makes it easier to attract the right clients and charge higher fees. Also, all that low dollar work is trapping her in a place where she does not perceive she has the time to do the work she was born to do. And the worst part is, the discounts she gives her clients is almost certainly part of what keeps them stuck right where they are.

I let her go gently, but I knew she would be ready the moment she made the decision to be ready. I didn't tell her that what she was doing, by undercharging her clients and keeping her message from the world, was stingy and not generous – but I wished I had. I didn't tell her an outside circumstance wasn't going to change her readiness. But I knew that even if she got to consistent income of over $5000/month without a book, there would be a reason that wasn't enough.

Then take Jim (you guessed it, not his real name either) –

- His book ambition has been a deep, dark secret. Not even his wife knows. (First clue.)
- He has a full time job that pays the bills, but he's unhappy. (Second clue.)
- He doesn't know what to write about, but he knows he has a lot to say. (Third clue.)
- He wants to quit his job and be a full time writer, but he's the primary breadwinner with kids in private school, so he'd need to be making over $8,000 a month.
- I asked him if he wanted to be a paid speaker, consultant or coach, and he explained he was an introvert and (right now) an engineer, and so that stuff didn't interest him.
- He wanted to write a book that would bring in all that revenue by itself. He could write about almost anything, and wanted to know what I thought would sell best so he could write about that. He knew he wasn't ready, but wanted me to tell him

what he had to do to be ready. (Fourth clue!)

I agreed he wasn't ready, and sent him off with the questions from Martha Beck that launched my business, starting with: *What do you lose track of time doing?*

What does this mean for you? It means you are ready if:

- You know in your heart you want to be an author.
- You have a message that will bring hope and healing to the world.
- You know you can be the change you want for your clients and readers.
- You aren't the kind of person who makes excuses, or at least believes them very long.
- You'd welcome money, but you don't see a book as a get rich quick scheme.
- You are already doing the work you love (at least some of the time) but want to do it in a bigger way, or reach more people.
- You aren't making the difference you want to make...*yet*!

Wondering if you are more like Sally than Jim? It's a reasonable question to ask. Drop me an email and we can schedule time for me to provide you with a custom analysis.

Have a question for The Author Incubator? Send me your ideas, comments and complaints. I want to know what you think. You can reach me at:

www.TheAuthorIncubator.com/contact-us

Chapter Six:
Don't Stop Me Now

Obstacles are those frightful things you see when you take your eyes off your goal.
~ Henry Ford

For many authors, the word "outline" inspires fear and loathing. There is a reason for that, in my opinion. Outlines are usually written from the land of "should." What should I put first? How should I structure this? What should I include and what should I leave out?

The word "should" comes from that right brain, masculine approach. And it works, at least a lot of the time. Unless it doesn't. Then, a very different process needs to be applied.

I don't want you to write an OUTline, I want you to write an INline. Outlines are about ego. InLines are a full expression of yourself as a servant. Yup, we are back to that again.

When you write an InLine, you are preparing to write your book in a way that will serve your reader and allow you to make a difference in their lives. Here's a good place to explain my theory on writing a book that makes a difference. A book that makes a difference has two key components to it.

First, it is a book with a message that has the potential to bring hope and healing to the world on a topic you are deliciously passionate about.

Second, it is a book that gets into people's hands and changes people's hearts. Not a book that sits in a box in your basement, or behind an unclicked link on Amazon.

I talked earlier about Brooke Castillo's book, *If I'm So Smart, Why Can't I Lose Weight?* That book has transformed my life and thousands of other lives. But if Brooke wrote that book and then stuffed it in a box in her storage unit, it wouldn't have been a book that makes a difference, despite its brilliance.

So just writing a book that has a powerful message of hope and healing isn't enough. You need to write it in a way that gets in people's hands.

In the Your Delicious Book program, I teach my authors-in-transformation lots of techniques to get their book in the world, but it all starts with the InLine. Your InLine starts by answering the question: *How do you want your reader to be different at the end of your book?* Everything in your book needs to be a part of the fabric that answers that question.

One of the problems I see most frequently is that many people come to me writing two or three or four books, and believing they are all one book. They want 27 different things for their reader, and in today's reading landscape, that's too much to ask. Your book needs to solve just one core problem.

Here are some before and after InLine makeovers I've done for clients:

Jimmy came to me wanting to write a book about confidence for men… well really for anyone… struggling with anything. What he had found was that the more confident he was, the easier it was for him to solve any problem he had and he wanted to share that. The problem is, most people don't come to Amazon looking for confidence books. So I asked him what kinds of problems he solves and he mentioned getting a promotion, setting boundaries with friends, and asking a girl out for a date. Great! Those were things we could work with.

Before: *The Confidence Manifesto*
After: A *series* of books aimed at specific challenges the reader may face.

The Confident Man's Guide to Getting the Promotion You Deserve
The Confident Man's Guide to Setting Boundaries with Friends & CoWorkers
The Confident Man's Guide to Asking a Beautiful Woman on a Date

Lizette came to me committed to writing a book about self-love and self-compassion. She had been through the wringer in her relationships with men – and with friends and bosses. She tried for years to change people, and it never worked. Then she stumbled upon the work of Byron Katie. She learned to separate out her business – the things she was responsible for, from other people's business and God's business. She wanted women her age to understand this but she also wanted to share this message with college girls. Here's where we ended up:

Before: *Self-Love: The Ultimate Tool for Happiness*

After: *Escape from Relationship Hell: How to Create a Life you Love*

Once you have your book narrowed down, ask yourself this: If you were explaining this to an alien, what details would you include?

Just make a simple list of everything you might include. Or better yet, make a list of questions, and you can essentially answer those questions as a way to write your book.

We'll use that information to make sure the InLine we write actually addresses the way we want your reader to be different at the end of the book. That means we are creating an InLine that is organic to what our ideal reader needs to know, not an outline that is forced based on what we think we should tell them.

THE DIFFERENCE PROCESS
STEP 6 – RELEASE YOUR BLOCKS

Start by making a list of everything that could go into your book. I usually recommend ten ideas per chapter, with five chapters for e-books and ten to twelve chapters for print books. Ideas, or discrete items, can include statistics, stories, case studies, quotes, images and exercises. Here's how I think of it:

- The best way to connect with your reader is through stories.
- The best way to establish credibility with your reader is through statistics.
- The best way to make your book *fun* is through cartoons and images.
- The best way to *leverage* your book is through worksheets and exercises with online downloads.

- The best way to demonstrate *results* is through graphics or infographics.

Next, sort your lists into categories (again, five for ebooks or 10-12 for print books). Try to put 5-15 items in each category. When I look at each item, I try to imagine it as a blog post or a Facebook post idea that I'm going to write later. For now, I'll sum it up in a few words or a sentence.

Here's how this chapter looked in my InLine

- Henry Ford quote
- InLine v. Outline
- Book that Makes a Difference Requirements
- Before & Afters
- Alien thing
- Release your block steps
- Q&A – formulas

When I sat down to write this chapter, I already knew what was going in it, and so it was very easy to write. I can talk about all those points in my sleep, because this is what I talk about all day long in my business. I never had to defeat the blank page, because those 7 "slugs" were a tip-off to 250 to 500 words of very accessible content. I like my chapters to land between 2500 and 5000 words (or between 10 and 20 pages double-spaced), so seven items works pretty well for me. I did have some other items in this chapter that got cut. They were:

- Common struggles and mistakes at this stage
- Schedule tool/syllabus story/working backwards

The first, I decided to cut because it just didn't feel right. I sort of mentioned them alongside all the other points. I didn't have a separate thing to say about it. The second just kind of bored me. I'm telling you the steps as we go, and as you will see, we work our InLines backwards. Instead of starting with what should go in the book, we sort of let the book tell us what it wants to be. It felt repetitive to explain that, so I dropped it.

Once you know what goes in each chapter (by grouping the items from your big list), write a sentence for each chapter to reflect how you want your reader to be different at the end of this chapter.

My statement for the whole book is: *I want my readers to know how to write a book that can change people's lives and make the author lots of money.* And my statement for this chapter is: *I want my reader to understand how to write an outline with ease that readers will connect with.*

Next to each chapter, I put a proposed page count or word count. This helps program the brain to send you the right amount of information and word flow.

If I were to tell you to write a chapter about writing a book outline, your brain will immediately start programming itself for about 5,000 words. But if I say, instead, *write a tweet about writing a book outline*, your brain knows, oh, this is like one fact or sentence about outlines. It's a totally different output. So by putting the page count or the word count next to each chapter, you are almost effortlessly making your book easier to write.

The last step for your InLine is to set a deadline for each chapter. It doesn't matter what the deadline is, just that you write the date next to that chapter and commit to writing it by that date. Put it in your calendar the day before, so if you haven't written it yet, you can pull an all-nighter if you have to.

If you aren't in a program like Your Delicious Book, I highly recommend having a keeper of the deadlines. This can be a friend or colleague, but they have to be someone who will hold you fully accountable and not go along with your story when you give an excuse.

Give them a minimum of $100 per deadline, and the name of a political candidate or cause you really hate. My sister Gina, is an active supporter of gun safety laws and has been since the tragic shooting at Sandy Hook Elementary in Newtown, Connecticut. If she was writing a 10 chapter book, I'd have her give me $1,000 in $100 bills. I'd put them in an envelope, and mark it NRA.

Every time she missed a deadline, one of her hard-earned, crisp, $100 bills would be mailed off to the good folks at the NRA, working against her. Knowing I was really going to do this would keep Gina's feet to the fire, to keep the promise she made to herself.

Inside the Author Incubator:
On Organization

Q: I've made the list of items I want to include in my book, and it's a hot mess. Is it possible I have a book with 57 very short chapters?

A: Truth is, it is possible. For my podcast, I've interviewed authors who have done books with books where there were 52 Keys to Unlocking some goal or another, and each "key" was its own chapter. So...maybe. But here's the deal, if you are having trouble creating an InLine, try to find a book that you can model your chapters after.

The key to getting your book done is in writing a smart outline (InLine). Setting achievable and desired completion dates. And sticking to them. Now you can make that easy, or you can up the challenge. Here are some formulas for non-overachievers. And yes, I can actually qualify as one sometimes!

Wanna make it easy to write your book? There are some really classic formats that you *might* be able to apply to your topic. For an ebook - let's say you want 5 chapters (plus a page or two intro and conclusion). Here are some ideas to make it easy on yourself. You get to be called an author, even if you take one of these easy template approaches to your first book. It's *not* cheating – it's being smart and efficient.

- INTERVIEWS – In 5 weeks, write 5 chapters, from 5 interviews:
- *Example*: Leyla Day's book on finding a job you love. She interviewed 8 people with jobs they loved about the journey they travelled to get there. EASY!
- STEPS (generally progressive steps) – In 5 weeks, write about 2 steps per week:
- *Example*: Ben Sands' book on financial freedom, he describes a cumulative approach to aligning your financial reality with your values and priorities, in other words maximizing the potential that your money will serve you, while minimizing the management hassles involved.
- LISTS OR COLLECTIONS - This is a lot like steps, but they don't have to be steps in an order - they can just be like *7 Habits of Highly Successful People* – where each habit gets a chapter, but the order doesn't matter.
- PROJECTS – in 5 weeks, create and write about 5 projects:

- I love project books. You don't have to know the end before you start writing. You just have to know the questions!
- MEMOIR EXAMPLE: Julie & Julia
- NONFICTION EXAMPLE: The Happiness Project
- STORIES - You can have something as simple as a theme - HOW YOU WANT YOUR READER TO BE DIFFERENT - and simply tell 5 stories on that theme.
- CLASSIC EXAMPLE: Chicken Soup for the Soul

Have a question for The Author Incubator? Send me your ideas, comments and complaints. I want to know what you think. You can reach me at:

www.TheAuthorIncubator.com/contact-us

CHAPTER SEVEN:
OH, WHAT A FEELING

You don't have to think about love; you either feel it or you don't.
— Laura Esquivel, Like Water for Chocolate

Finally! It's time to write your book. Remember how I said starting by writing your book was the *number one* mistake first time authors make? Well, if you have gotten this far, then you have earned the right to write. Most writing done without this level of preparation is a waste of time. And *that* is what causes the proverbial writer's block and procrastination. Your Inner Author is protecting you from doing something dumb. *Three cheers for writer's block.*

But now, you are ready. You have released the blocks. You have an InLine with all the information that's going into each chapter. You know how long each chapter will be, and when you will write it. And most importantly, you are writing with the heart of a servant to your reader, whose life will be changed by reading your book.

There is one, teeny, tiny, tedious but critically important step left to make your writing smooth sailing so you can write from a place of joy and ease.

How can you write your book with ease and joy? You have to start by establishing your author feeling state scale. I know it's kind of boring, but the payoff is massive. Not having this tool is the reason so many people have a love-hate relationship with writing. What if you choose to just have a love-love relationship. You *can*, you know.

And here's why it matters. The energy that goes into the book is the energy that comes out of it. Have you ever read Tim Ferris' books? He is amazing and the books are amazing, but dear God, I don't know about you, but I feel like I'm hopped up on speed when I read them. I suspect Tim lives his life with that intensity, and it comes through in living color through his books, even in a subtle and energetic way. So when you write from your highest place as an author, that feeling will come through for your readers – and you readers will be connecting with the entire energetic experience, not just the words in your book.

The way we do this at The Author Incubator is with a tool called the Author Feeling State scale, or your AFS. Your AFS ranges from -10 to +10, and you can follow along with the exercise in this chapter to create your own scale and calibrate your AFS accordingly.

When you sit down to write your book, identify your AFS.

If you are between +6 and +10, get the hell out of the way and get writing! Huzzah!

If you are between +1 and +5, you have three good options:

1. Acknowledge where you are, and ask your Inner Author what it would take to get to a +6 or higher. Sometimes this means reorganizing the kids toys, taking the dog for a walk, playing a great song, or making a hot beverage. Whatever nurtures you.

2. Acknowledge where you are, and make a *conscious* decision to "white knuckle" it. This is counter-intuitive, but it works. Here's what I say to my clients: "You are

a smart woman. You got through school and wrote papers you didn't want to and you did just fine. Maybe you didn't get an A on every paper, but you survived. Explain to your Inner Author you know she doesn't want to come out and play right now and that's fine, but you are going to continue writing anyway. Explain that she can bitch, whine and complain, but you have a deadline." When you do this, an *amazing* thing happens a lot of the time – but you can't do this to manipulate your Inner Author as a strategy (she's very sensitive about that sort of thing). If you *truly* commit to not wrestling with your Inner Author, and believe 100% in white knuckling it, very often your Author Feeling State gets an automatic boost, and white knuckling can evolve into writing with joy and ease. But again, you cannot strictly *will* this into happening. Just be open to her coming out to play if she decides to. This is the option I recommend when you really are on a deadline and you just *have* to get it done.

3. Finally, instead of writing you can work on other book tasks, like making lists of people to interview, organizing quotes and placing them into the chapters they go in, grabbing bits and bobs you have written in other places and dropping them into the manuscript, editing previous chapters, writing your bio or your acknowledgements, etc. These are not strictly writing, but they are the other essential pieces of your book that you need to handle for your book, and it's a great use of the +1 - +5 states.

You will know if you are a 0 or below because you will not be able to write. So here's what to do. See if you can shift into a positive state, by asking yourself what you want to do right then – and do it. Set a timer for 15 minutes, and check in with yourself and see if your AFS is moving. Is it improving or worsening? If it's getting better, but not into positive territory yet, give yourself another 15 minutes and try again.

If you are between a -6 and a -10, *call a doctor*! Seriously! Okay, call a book doctor or a friend. This is a huge opportunity! I get soo, sooo, soooooo excited when my authors have the blessing of a -6 to -10. This is writer's block! It's the moment you have been waiting for. It is a zone of magic and enchantment.

Yes, I understand you are confused right now. A book coach who is pro writer's block?!?! What does it mean?

Well, as I have explained already, writer's block is a sign from your Inner Author that you are off track, but there is more! Your Inner Author is trying to get your attention, because she knows you are ready for a major breakthrough. If you keep going the way you are going, you are going to miss it. But like any good quest, the reward only comes after you complete the challenge. This is your gauntlet. Ignore it, and you don't get the prize. Walk through the fire, and...*Blammo*! Wizard-level Achieved!

This is the moment you have asked for and waited for. Can you, and *will* you, be brave enough to accept the challenge? If you can stay with your Inner Author and get the secret message, you will be bequeathed riches beyond your imagination.

Let me tell you a story about one of my clients with Writer's Block. She was working on a book called Happiness Junkie, and in her book, there was a chapter about Practice which had her all wrapped around the axel. She could not get through the chapter, could not even skip it and move on. She was paralyzed. She knew what she *wanted* to say about practice. It was hard. Stick with it. Yadda yadda yadda. But it would not come out of her fingertips.

She called me for a coaching session, right at the critical moment, and I was able to access her Inner Author. The truth was, this chapter was *never* about practice! Her Inner Author was trying to tell her that no one needs another author to tell them they should *practice*. It's not helpful, it's preachy, and it's not being of service. The rest of her book was "InLine" but this particular element was "Out-of-line." In fact, Caren confessed to me, she didn't even really like practice very much herself. So of course her Inner Author was balking. Inner Authors do not like *shoulds*!

What her Inner Author told me was that this chapter was supposed to be about resistance to practice instead. No one needs another lecture on how to practice or why it's important. They need to understand *why* they don't want to practice! Her experience with Writer's Block was mirroring what she needed to be teaching, not ignoring. Caren was a special messenger, and yet she was refusing to pick up the package for delivery. But when she got really quiet, the answer was clear and the writing, smooth sailing.

Go pick up a copy of her book and read chapter 8. I think you'll see the special magic this experience of Writer's Block brought to the world, all because Caren was willing to listen to the truth, and not try to fight or ignore her way out of it.

THE DIFFERENCE PROCESS
STEP 7 – ESTABLISH YOUR AUTHOR FEELING STATE

The Author Feeling State tool is used to identify your thoughts about working on your book. When you create your book, you should always be in the positive zone (otherwise you are white knuckling it and probably wasting time). If you are in the negative zone, your only job as an author is to move from negative to positive territory. It runs from -10, which is total writers block, to +10, which is being so in the writing zone your book is practically writing itself. Zero is neutral. You need to use this scale as a gauge. Before you start writing, you need to identify where you are on the scale, and proceed according to a plan. This will keep writers block from ever derailing you on your book journey.

To get started, identify a -10 story. Think of a time when you were totally blocked from working on a project. Any project, not necessarily writing your book, that was important to you. Describe how you felt, and most importantly, identify at least one thought you were thinking at the time. Something like, "I'm never going to finish this book." Or, "I have no good ideas."

Next, tell a +10 story. This doesn't have to be about your book. It could be a story about any time you were writing, even if it was a birthday card for your mom. Think of the last you're your writing just flowed out of you. Describe that time. How did you feel in your body? What physical sensations were there? And most importantly, what were one or two thoughts you had, like, "I'm actually a pretty good writer," or, "This blog post just has to be written, just like this!"

Do the same for 0, -5 and +5. We'll talk about how we will use this tool in our next session. For now, capture the thoughts and feelings you have at these five key points on the Author Feeling State scale.

Here's a sample Author Feeling State Scale from one of my clients.

AUTHOR FEELING STATE SCALE

Once you know how to calibrate your Author Feeling State (AFS) compass, you have the tools to invite your Inner Author out to play when it's time to write. Remember, your Inner Author is on your side. She wants you to write the book you were born to write, and she will stop you when you are off track. This is great news! You don't need me or any other expert to tell you what's right for your book. Your Inner Author already knows, because she already wrote this book!

FEELING STATE	STORY (CIRCUMSTANCES)	FEELING(S)	THOUGHT(S)
-10	Writing for a boring consulting job	Frustrated Impatient Upset/angry Sad	I don't want to do this. I'm wasting my time just to make some money. This has no meaning to me.
-5	Writing newsletters for my coaching business	Forced (a bit) Inauthentic Frustrated to get started	I have to send one out every month. I don't like writing the how-to's Subject matter didn't flow naturally (because of the "have to" thought)

0	Correspondence; customer service issues or requests, or contract negotiations.	Ease Satisfied Productive	I write good letters. It comes easy for me to make a case, argue a point, with rational facts. Most often they have produced positive results.
+5	One or two newsletters	Clear Spontaneous Honest	These were more personal; less "how to." I was moved to write by my emotions.
+10	A research paper I did in undergrad.	Curious Interested Engaged Excited Meaningful	I really wanted to know what the research would reveal. I love arranging and organizing my findings. I personalize my introduction (intention) and conclusion to my own personal experience.
	A thank you letter to my family.	Honest Grateful Expressive	I wanted to communicate gratitude and love. I spoke personally to each family member. It is daring (feeling vulnerable) to open up and express unspoken feelings.
	Writing the test chapter for my book.	Excited (nervous) Engaged Challenging Accomplished Proud	I had an idea that was easy to formulate on paper. I enjoy organizing and arranging my content. I love the idea of finishing, accomplishing the project

Inside the Author Incubator:
On Doubts

Q: I am writing, but I have to tell you, I'm not sure it's any good! My third grade teacher told me I was a terrible writer, and I think she might have been right. How do I know if I have it in me to be an author? Maybe this isn't for me. I don't want to embarrass myself.

A: Authors who are in the middle of writing almost always have doubts. I'm hearing a lot of you dealing with doubt and uncertainty in the middle part of the writing process – is this good enough? Am I good enough? *Please* know this is a normal part of the process and just your little gremlin or inner lizard coming up. Seth Godin has a terrific little book called *The Dip*. In it, he explains when to quit and when to keep going.

Every new project starts out exciting and fun. Then it gets harder and less fun, until it hits a low point – really hard, and not much fun at all. And then you find yourself asking if the goal is even worth the hassle. Maybe you're in a Dip – a temporary setback that will get better if you keep pushing. But maybe it's really a Cul-de-Sac, which will never get better, no matter how hard you try. What really sets superstars apart from everyone else is the ability to escape dead ends quickly, while staying focused and motivated when it really counts.

If you have gotten this far, this attack of self-doubt is not a dead end, it's just a dip. If you have a servant's heart and an ideal reader you know you can help, and if you know in your heart you are supposed to write this book, then all this hullabaloo about your third grade teacher is just that. A story that keeps you from passing through the dip.

I'll give you the same advice I give my authors day after day: Don't look back. Keep writing *FORWARD.*

Have a question for The Author Incubator? Send me your ideas, comments and complaints. I want to know what you think. You can reach me at:

www.TheAuthorIncubator.com/contact-us

CHAPTER EIGHT:
TAKING CARE OF BUSINESS

Whenever you feel an impulse to perpetrate a piece of exceptionally fine writing, obey it—whole-heartedly—and delete it before sending your manuscript to press. Murder your darlings.
~ Arthur Quiller-Couch, On the Art of Writing

I have consistently found that the most successful authors are those who write the entire book from start to finish, without going back and editing. Going back and editing while you are writing causes two problems. The first problem it causes is that it creates an almost endless loop of perfectionism. The manuscript is never right, and this rewriting cycle feeds upon itself.

Have you ever tried painting? My best friend's daughter and I went to a painting class together once. In the class, we were supposed to paint a jungle scene in the style of Henri

Rousseau. Sofia was six at the time, and she is a born artist. She was painting castles and unicorns better than anything I could do before she started school. When the instructor showed us Rousseau's work, Sofia instantly had an idea for her painting – and got straight to work mixing colors and slapping them on canvas.

I was off in a corner trying to draw on the canvas with a pencil to make sure I got everything "right" before I "ruined" the canvas with paint. (I bet you see where this is going!)

When I finally started painting, Sofia had already finished, and was walking around the class giving feedback to students with the teacher, who was fully wrapped around her finger at this point. I would paint a bush and then go back and repaint it, and try again – over and over. I couldn't ever get it to look on the canvas the way it did in my mind's eye.

Of course what was in my mind's eye was Rousseau! I wanted my picture to look just like his. How did he get the shading under each of the leaves? Did I need a smaller brush? What was I doing wrong?

Sofia, on the other hand, never went back to touch things up until her entire painting was done. And then she started adding pink hearts to the orange tree because *she could*!

All of her editing came at the end, while I was viciously attacking myself through the whole process. Her picture was her own interpretation of Rousseau, pink hearts and all! Mine was a really, really, really bad attempt at copying a master. I'll let you guess whose picture actually looked better.

What was worse, wasn't even that my painting wasn't very good, it was that I felt kinda crappy about myself while my teacher, little miss Sofia, was on cloud nine. She was *an artist*! I was a failure.

This is the emotional cycle I see editing brings into most of my authors' hearts when they are editing as they write. Now this isn't to say you will publish an unedited book. Of course, I'm not advocating that. But what I am advocating is that your Inner Author doesn't really love being critiqued while she is working. She's got stuff to say, and when you jump in and beat her up, she doesn't feel free and light and ready to share.

Your Inner Author also doesn't need you to coddle her, but the relationship needs to be nurtured. And that's where the Nurture Your Manuscript step comes in. It's editing, in a thoughtful way.

The second problem that happens when you edit while you are writing is that you may change as you write. Your first chapter will sound a little different than your fifth. As your voice develops, you will be better able to edit those early chapters at the end of the process of writing, because you will be so much clearer on who you are, and what you want to say.

Take my client, Joe. His book started as a two-author collaboration, but halfway through the book, Joe's co-author dropped out. The first half of the book was written with a shared voice of "we," but the second half was Joe on his lonesome. This led to a significant rewrite and changing or deleting a lot of the stories in the earlier book that had belonged to his co-author. Had Joe been editing all along, he would have wasted a lot of effort cleaning up those early chapters. Since he was my client, he knew this, and resisted the urge to rewrite even when he and his co-author parted ways. We waited until the entire book was finished. Then, when he went to clean up those early chapters, the work was significant – *but he only had to do it once.*

Editing mid-draft is a way to hold your Inner Author back. Writing forward is giving your book the floor to express itself, knowing you are still in charge, and you won't publish until you are ready.

Participants in my Your Delicious Book program are paired with a developmental editor during their writing process. The editor's role is, in part, accountability to deadlines and accountability to ensure the book stays on track. The relationship between the author and reader is clear, and every sentence is designed to move the reader to the place where the author wants the reader to arrive at the end of the book.

If you are going off course in our program, the developmental editor will course-correct without you needing to dive back into the manuscript too deeply. Mostly, you reset and continue to write forward, knowing you may need to revisit earlier chapters at the end. This way, our developmental editors protect our authors from getting to the end of the manuscript and realizing they have written the wrong book.

Make sure you have someone who understands what you are trying to do with your book, who can give you regular feedback, so you don't write yourself into a corner. Getting feedback like this is tricky, because generally editors want to edit. They want to be "helpful," but generally helpful without a shared mind and purpose can often throw your Inner Author off the scent. It's a tricky balance, but my advice is always to go with your gut. If it doesn't feel like your editor "gets" you, try someone else.

I often request a partial edit of a chapter or so, to see if there is a good fit, before committing to the whole project. Do this test run, even if it's a friend who is doing it for free, so you have an easy "Get out of jail free" card. Don't feel beholden to share the whole book with them if it doesn't feel good. You don't even have to tell them it's any kind of test, or that you are looking for an editor for your entire book. Just tell them the type of feedback you are looking for, and see what they deliver. *Then ask your Inner Author if she is a fan.*

Types of Editors

One thing that's important to understand is that there are several different types of editors. At The Author Incubator, we pretty much stick with a Developmental Editor to work with during the writing process, and a copy editor and/or proofreader once your manuscript is complete. Sometimes, this is the same person, but it can be very helpful to engage a new set of eyes in a proofreader.

A proofreader is a pretty easy concept to understand, and it's the step that most authors think of when they think of "editing." They check for grammar, spelling, formatting, sentences, subject-verb agreement, punctuation, and voice. They go through every inch of a manuscript, word by word, line by line. They are looking for the mistakes that may have been missed during previous edits, but they aren't looking strategically at your manuscript to see if it accomplishes the goals you set out for the book. That's the developmental editor's job.

Developmental editors keep the book moving forward, ensuring your voice is consistent, and that you are meeting your writing goals. They are checking to make sure you are doing what you said you wanted to do, and they are checking to make sure your reader can follow your logic. They notice and observe where you go off on a tangent or skip a big step. They wave a flag with varying degrees of intensity. If they catch a typo they may also point it out, but they aren't really looking for grammar or punctuation. They are reviewing your book at a higher, and more strategic level.

Maybe more importantly, our developmental editors are like personal trainers. Given human nature, if you work out alone, you might well go to the gym and do a sort of lazy 30 minutes on the treadmill followed by a round on the weight machines. Ok. Whereas if you do the same work out with a trainer standing next to you, you'll increase the incline on the treadmill, run faster, and then lift more weight? Developmental editors work just that way. They are your stand-in for your ideal reader. Instead of hiding alone in your Bat Cave secretly writing away, you know you are going to share 5 to 20 pages a week with your developmental editor, so you will want them to be of a reasonable quality.

Our editors know that too, and so in addition to be editors, they are book coaches who can respond to the hiccups that come along the road of writing a book. These hiccups can look like very obvious circumstantial reasons why you just can't finish. Here are some of the obstacles my authors have had to overcome to get their books done:

- We found a total of four baby squirrels in my tackroom, obviously orphaned or abandoned, but the nearest wildlife center where they could be properly cared for is an hour away. Needless to say, that chewed up most of the day.

- Five days before deadline: sick dog in hospital. Five days in bed with flu, and the Mac even crashed the night before deadline!

- When I get into the flow, I am focused and don't hear or see anything going on around me. This felt like benign neglect to both my children and husband, who would then go into overdrive to try and get my attention.

- Mom fell over 4th of July weekend, and we went to ER to have her checked out.

- I had 12 neighborhood kids in and out, a construction crew building a room addition and painting our house, and a three-week mystery illness that had me bedridden, so yes, craziness. I thought it would be easier in the summer when I didn't have to focus on homeschooling.
- Teenagers who started saying: you never have time for us.
- I traveled a couple of times, and I've got my medical condition to deal with every day.
- I was putting my house on the market, and got sucked into very full-time general contracting!

Just the act of *knowing* their developmental editor was there, holding space for their work, made it significantly easier for these authors to finish despite so harrowing circumstances. And there will *always* be harrowing circumstances – that's why you get to call yourself a hero/ine when your book is complete!

A Brief Philosophical Diversion (optional reading)

I'm not going to go TOO deeply into this here. In case you are curious, there is a philosophical concept behind the way we have our Development Editing team set up. Back when I was studying for my Ph.D., I became very interested in a French scholar named Jacques Lacan. In the psychoanalytic theory of Lacan, there is a concept called "The Gaze." He talks about the moment when a child first sees himself in a mirror, and recognizes the difference between himself and a reflection of himself.

I'm not looking back at my grad school notes here, but the way I remember it, this happens at about 18 months old, and creates the new awareness that one can be viewed. The crux of The Gaze is that it's pretty nerve wracking to the toddler, because you are realizing you are separate from your mother and… well…*alone.* The Gaze creates a longing or a desire for the unattainable object of desire known to philosophy wonks like me as "*objet petit a*" or "the other."

Okay, why are we suddenly having a lesson in French psychoanalytic theory?

Well, because in this case we are leveraging that desire for the other by using a developmental editor. Your editor fills that longing because otherwise, the longing or what feel like fear that everyone is going to hate your book, can overwhelm you into a state of non-finishing.

If you want to know more about what Lacan says about this – or better yet – where Melanie Kline's analysis of how this psychic enemy creates self-sabotage, shoot me a note at info@TheAuthorIncubator.com, and we can dish post modern philosophy together!

And if I've lost you in all this psycho-babble, no worries! Just know that developmental editors who can hold this space for you in a thoughtful way will make you MUCH more likely to finish your book, just like great personal trainers make you MUCH more likely to reach your physical goals.

THE DIFFERENCE PROCESS
Step 8 – Nurture Your Manuscript

Nurturing your manuscript isn't just about editing. There are some other ways you can move your manuscript closer to you reaching your goals. Here are three examples of moving your manuscript forward when you feel like neither writing nor editing:

Nurture Secret #1
Go through your manuscript and notice anyone you quote. If they are alive, find their contact information and reach out to them for "permission" to use their quote. Now don't panic, according to fair use doctrine, in most cases you don't need permission to quote someone. It is a nice gesture, and not only that, it gives you an opportunity to let that person know you are writing a book. This is a great way to open the door to ask for a testimonial blurb (which we call Advance Praise). Make sure you

review their books on Amazon and/or Goodreads before you reach out. Once they approve your use of the quote, you can mention how much you would appreciate it if they would consider giving you advance praise for your book, and if they are open to it you can send them an Early Reader copy of the book before it goes to press. *Hat tip to my client Jill Farmer, who actually taught me this one herself when we were working on her book.*

Nurture Secret #2

Have you noticed how throughout this book I have encouraged you to email me, or to go to www.TheAuthorIncubator.com and sign up for the free 4-part video series which goes with this book? The truth is, I really want you to email me – and to watch those videos. I love talking to people about their books (it's really pretty much all I want to do), and I made that video series to share some critical information because I see authors making mistakes all the time that kill me. Their books are great, but they can't make a difference – because no one can find them!

But, in addition to being completely and utterly in alignment with my deepest desire, which is to help you write a book that matters, these are "lead generation" prompts. I want to be in a dialogue with you, because someday you may want to work with me, or you may know someone who does.

Remember how I told you I had spent $20,000 with authors Martha Beck and Brooke Castillo? Well, it all started with the initial contacts to the author I made while I was reading their book.

This part is really hard for me to share, but I really want you to understand the power you have to change someone's life. I'm about to share with you the actual email I wrote to Brooke when I finished her book. This is the original, with no edits (eek, typos and all), and it's really hard for me to read now. In it, you can hear how desperate I was and how hard I was trying to cover it up. I was so scared and I really needed help. I'm pretty much begging her to take my money.

From: Angela Lauria alauriam@aim.com
Subject: Coach Question
Date: April 19, 2007 at 12:33:54 AM
To: brooke@coach4weight.com

Hi Brooke,

Thanks so much for your amazing work. I gained 85 lbs with my first child (born about a year ago) and haven't been able to lose the weight. Since I pride myself of being "smart," the title of your book caught my attention and it's definitely one of the most inspiring books I've ever read. I've been working my way through the excersizes you lay out and I've lost about 20 lbs in 2 months. I still have plenty to lose but I feel great already. I also went to the doctor and learned I have post-partum hypothyroidism and Polycystic Ovarian Syndrome, which probably isn't helping my case! The great news is I am eating less than ever and don't feel like I am on a diet. Just being conscious is making a huge difference in the quantity and quality of food I eat. I am registered for your Lake Tahoe retreat, but between now and then I'd love to supercharge my weight release efforts with a great coach. I'd love to work with you directly because I know you could help get me past some difficult

hurdles in this journey. I believe this
process would be rewarding for us both.
Thanks for considering working with me,
Angela Lauria
202-230-4444

I don't know if you can hear it, but I was *really, really* selling myself there. I spent almost a month crafting that email, because I was sure she was going to say no. I was a hot mess. Everything in my life was collapsing, but I wanted her to pick me as her client – and I really didn't feel good enough. I can hear that in the sort of corporate, bullshitty tone I wrote it in.

Do you get the power there? That's what your book can do – make your prospects beg to work with you.

"Thanks for considering working with me."

Really, that's my last line?

How about: "If you double your prices, I'll still say yes." Oh wait, and I would have too. If she said yes, I was prepared to take a home equity line on my house to work with her. That's how committed I was to selling HER on working with ME.

That is why you want to nurture your manuscript – and your ideal reader, who is dying for you to come into their life – with lead generation prompts like the ones I have here.

Nurture Secret #3
Your Special Sauce…..Mmm Delicious!
Your Special Sauce says how your approach is unique, and how is your book going to be distinct from others on your subject. For me, my special sauce is "The D.I.F.F.E.R.E.N.C.E. Process." Now listen, I'm not going to pretend I'm the first book coach who suggested you identify your ideal reader, or that you find a great editor. I get it. A lot of this isn't rocket science, and hardly new ideas. But what I did on my own was organize my ideas in order to solve the most pressing problem on your ideal reader's mind. (And it may well be a pressing problem for other people too – but for your ideal reader it's *the* most pressing.) My ideal reader doesn't really care about money. I mean look, they have to eat, and money is nice, but my ideal reader knows, their life will be meaningless if they don't give back and help people with the lessons they have learned.

Just now, as I was writing this chapter I got a call from a prospect, who became a client by the end of the call. She told me how she had been a top student, and landed a great career. She always worked hard and went to church. But somehow, she ended up with a string of abusive relationships. She'd been beaten, robbed, and even shot. She knows the reason she is still alive today is to help other women to survive. It's not even like she just "wants" to do this. She has been called to stand and serve. Sure, she could write a book without me, but could she be *absolutely sure* it would make the difference she needs to make, to give her 10 year recovery from being shot by a partner worth that torture?

That's why I created the DIFFERENCE Process. It's my special sauce. No one else does it, and no one else *can* do it. Yes, many of the steps might be similar, but the process is my intellectual property. And you can create some intellectual property of your own during this nurture phase, too, which could grow into a sustainable means of living on work that changes lives.

Your Special Sauce could be:

- A Process with steps
- A Quiz

- A Method described through an acronym
- A framework
- A system
- A plan
- A map
- A blueprint
- A combination of things
- Your Special Sauce MUST be:
- Nameable
- Memorable
- Copyrightable or Trademarkable
- Specific
- Something someone else can teach

Give it a go! And if you get stuck, remember you can always reach out to me directly for a strategy session, and we'll see if working together might be the thing to shake it loose for you!

Inside the Author Incubator:
On Critiques

Q: Should I join a writing circle or critique group to share my writing?

A: I get this question a lot. Authors often create a first draft, and then they feel like they need feedback, so they join a writer's group. They get to the writer's group, read a small section to a random cross section of other insecure writers who probably don't have great Author Coaches, and then get critical, or even hateful feedback. Or well-meaning, but non-strategic feedback that sends them down the rabbit hole.

If you happen to know your Myers Briggs profile and you are an INFP – make a promise to me, yourself and all that is holy in this world never, ever, ever to go to ANYTHING with the word critique in it. That's not for you. You don't need to thicken your skin. You skin is perfect just how it is. And you have some holy magic to share with this world and it is going to be hard enough for you to do what you were put on this planet to do. You don't need a bunch of ENTJ jerks like me to send you into a spiral of self-doubt. Skip it. Pay someone you love, or find a friend you trust, and share your writing that way.

For all 15 other MBTI types… you've got a choice here. Before you make it, remember any feedback you get is going to tell you a lot more about the giver of the feedback than it will about you.

Our managing editor, Kate Makled, explains it this way: "When I participated in groups, I often got the "dumb it down" feedback. One time, I was told I needed to dial my "sophisticated *New York Times* vocabulary" down and write for about a sixth grade level to make my stuff more accessible. (Dear 22 year old self, you were in the wrong f'ing environment)."

As long as you know that you can separate the good advice from the bad, it's possible you'll have a good experience – or even make a new friend. Can you be successful without it? Sure. My advice, honestly and truly, is to steer clear of these sorts of groups. I'd limit myself to participating in paid groups with a trained facilitator, and I'd ask what the ground rules are for participation before I join. If possible, go to a trial session before you make a commitment, to see what it's like. I've never found groups like this helpful for my clients. I put them in the category of things people do to keep themselves busy and small while pretending they really want to be a published author. That means these groups are for people who want to WANT to write a book – not for difference-makers like you.

*Have a question for The Author Incubator?
Send me your ideas, comments and
complaints. I want to know what you think.
You can reach me at:*

www.TheAuthorIncubator.com/contact-us

CHAPTER NINE:
PUTTING IT TOGETHER

Putting it together...
Piece by Piece-
Only way to make a work of art.
Every moment makes a contribution,
Every little detail plays a part.
Having just a vision's no solution,
Everything depends on execution:
Putting it together-
That's what counts!
~Stephen Sondheim, Sunday in the Park

Now you've got your manuscript done, but how do you get your books in the hands of readers? There is no way around it, you are going to need a publisher. Even if that publisher is, well, you! One of the most important decisions you'll make around your book is how to publish. It's normal to be overwhelmed by all the choices and jargon in the publishing world, and pick what seems easiest.

I've been working with authors since 1994. Some of them have made the *New York Times* Bestseller list, and some never even finished their book. Want to know the difference between the two? Many people would guess it was the publisher they went with and that's the deciding factor, but they would be wrong. The real difference is that authors who understand their business model and know *why* they are writing, and what the completed book will do for them, are always more successful. It's really that simple.

Once you understand *why* you are writing, picking a publisher will come naturally. There is no right or wrong answer. The reason it's confusing – and the book industry is *really* confusing for first-time authors – is because the onus is on the author to understand their own business model and pick the publishing method that fits. Many first-time authors, however, don't know where to start, so they choose a path without really understanding the option or the consequences!

One of my clients, Julie, was new to writing and to life coaching. She held off building her new coaching practice, and instead worked her tail feather off for two years to get her manuscript accepted by Penguin Books. She was thrilled when it was published. While her advance was small – just $5,000 – she figured with the Penguin name and the quality of her book – plus a celebrity foreword, she'd earn out the advance in no time, and have a monthly royalty check that would pay off a new car.

About three months after Julie's book was published, she started to understand what the other publishers who turned her down were talking about. She had sold about 800 books, was frustrated with her publisher for not doing more marketing, her books were no longer in book stores, and she wished she had never signed with Penguin in the first place. If she had to do it all over again, Julie says, she would have self-published the day she finished her manuscript, and spent those two years building her business, instead of begging to be published by a major publishing house.

My client Lisa was in a similar boat. New to coaching and writing, Lisa put a proposal together and shopped it around. Her vision was clear, she wanted a TV show, and this book was the corner stone to an elaborate national press strategy. When she met with agents and publishers, she explained her goal and said, "I have a proposal here, but I'd like to know what kind of a book sounds interesting to you."

Like Julie, Lisa got a small advance, $3,500. Unlike Julie, Lisa wasn't writing the book of her dreams, instead she was writing a book that her research indicated would make it easy for her to get free publicity. Lisa's goal for this book was to start building her platform, and having St. Martin's Press behind her helped with the bookings. It was well worth the eighteen-month wait. Lisa isn't sure how many books she's sold, "It's not very many," she admits. But she was recently booked on *Good Morning America* and quoted in the *New York Times*.

The point of those stories is that every type of publishing has options, but if you don't understand your business strategy, you'll be likely to be unhappy with your publisher or your book's performance, if you don't start out with the end in mind. It won't surprise you to know, this is significantly easier said than done!

Many of my clients are just starting their coaching practices, and their goal is to establish expertise and maybe build their subscriber list.

Ultimately, these activities will help them get a major advance with a traditional publisher if that's a direction they want to go, but they don't have the time to spend trying to get a publisher or waiting the years it takes to go through the standard process. To short-cut the system, many of my clients work hard to get a book out within a year of opening the doors of their business, either through self-publishing or another alternative such as our Your Delicious Book program.

What Does a Publisher Do?

Whether you intend to self-publish, work with a traditional publisher, or work with a specialty publisher, this is what needs to happen to get your book out:

Editing – Whether you work with a development editor or you hire a freelance editor, you will need to work with an objective third party to make sure your manuscript is in its best form before going to print.

Art Direction –In any big project like a book, having a single person holding the vision of the look, feel, and branding in your book is essential to have clean, consistent design, inside and out. If you are self-publishing, you may end up as your own art director, but beware – this role is deceptively difficult.

Cover Design – There is a great deal of science that goes in to book cover design. After all, people don't read your book before they buy it – the cover is usually all they have to go on.

Interior Design – Someone needs to pick a typeface for the text that is not only readable, but fits the style of your book. That person is your interior designer. They'll have other responsibilities too, especially if you have worksheets, illustrations, or tips.

Production Management – Getting your book printed is a critical step in the process. Someone will need to find the best printer, whether it's print-on-demand or a more traditional approach. Sourcing the paper and managing the printer is all part of production management.

Registration – Your publisher will also provide you with a unique ISBN number to identify your book as well as a Library of Congress Control number to help make it easy for your book to get found.

Planning – A "managing editor" (probably you if you are self-publishing) needs to keep track of the whole project.

Distribution – How does the book go from the printer into a customer's hands? Someone is going to need to manage relationships with large and independent book stores, online book outlets, Baker & Taylor and/or Ingram for ordering, and specialty distribution relationships.

Selling – Publishers will send catalogs and sales staff to libraries, schools, and bookstores. If you are self-publishing, this step is likely to get skipped – unless it's central to your business model.

Promotional Copy – One of the many overlooked aspects of book writing is the jacket copy and other short summaries of the books used on Amazon.com or in catalogs. In about 100 words, the promotional copywriter has to sell the book's sizzle.

What your publisher will *not* do is marketing. Many people are under the misimpression that publishers do this. Unless you are J.K. Rowling, they don't. Publishers have marketing staffs that send out a few review copies of your book, and may dash off a press release as part of their seasonal catalog announcement, but sadly, those marketing techniques are pretty ineffective. To sell your book, you'll need to build a list of fans, online and off. That's in your hands. Free publicity is one part of the equation, social media, search engine optimization, and email marketing are just a few of the others.

A View of Traditional Publishing

Many people, like Julie and Lisa, feel anything less than a contract with a major publisher, isn't worth pursuing. If your heart and gut say the same, here are some things you should know.

Getting picked up by a traditional publisher is a bit like winning the lottery. Authors must first secure an agent to pitch their manuscript. Finding an agent can be daunting and grueling. Agents only make money when their clients do, but this means they are often very selective about their clients. It's not unusual to reach out to 20 or 30 agents with query letters before finding one that is willing to take on a new author.

Agents will pitch your idea, but only after you have created a detailed book proposal with sample chapters, a marketing plan, and more. Creating a good proposal can take months, as can the pitching process. For many authors, it doesn't happen. If a first-time author *does* get their idea picked up, the publisher will buy the rights and take complete control over the content, design, distribution, in-store promotion, and publication date. In fact, a publisher can even decide to "kill" a book and not publish it at all. Once the publisher receives the manuscript, it can take months or years before it's printed. During that time editors, designers, marketers, and other experts are working on all aspects of your book.

With traditional publishing, most authors get a payment in advance for expected royalties from their work – usually $1,500 – $10,000 for new, non-fiction authors – and they don't have to spend any money on the production and distribution of the book. For many authors, it's the allure of the publisher's bearing the majority of the financial risk that attracts writers to publishing with traditional houses.

There is a cost to authors when publishers bear the risk. The author gives away the rights to the book for some period of time – generally five to seven years – and receives a small royalty for each book that's sold, usually 5-8% of the retail price. Royalties are only received after the publisher recoups all their costs, including the advance if there was one.

Many authors are shocked to discover publishers do very little to market or promote the book outside of asking for reviews and getting bookstore shelf space.

There is a thrill to being accepted by a traditional publisher and a credibility bump that is nearly unrivaled. One of the top reasons for pursuing traditional publishing is the desire for validation and legitimacy. This desire shouldn't be minimized. It's important to recognize what percentage of your interest in traditional publishing is to get that validation, so you can export your assumptions about how best you can get the approval you seek.

The Many Faces Of Self- Publishing

Self-publishing, as an alternative to the legacy commercial publishers, is one that has dramatically expanded in popularity over the past 5 years. Today, there are many successful self-published authors who did not have the wait and struggle associated with traditional publishing. The cost is not insignificant. As a self-publisher, authors work with a company or freelancers to accomplish the same tasks a publisher would tackle over the year or so they'd spend with your manuscript.

Technically, there are many ways to "self-publish." To truly self-publish, you'll be responsible for everything from getting the ISBN, to cover design, line-editing, interior design, Library of Congress registration and much more. You can hire people to do each of those pieces separately, or hire one person to do all those steps but if the ISBN is in your name – it's Self-Published. The problem with self-publishing is it requires someone, like a life coach, to become a marketing and publishing expert on top of their coaching profession.

If that seems like too much work, you can find an author-funded publisher (sometimes called a Vanity publisher) to manage the process of getting your book published and distributed. When you self-publish on your own or with an author-funded publisher, you retain all rights and royalties in exchange for paying up front to have your book published as a service.

Without the checks and balances of a traditional publishing company, a self-published book can also generally be spotted for its poor design and editing. That's why picking the right author-funded publisher can make the difference between a success and a failure. All the money you spend on the front end, can be recouped if your book is done well. As always, it's a balance between risk and reward.

Often, people tell me they don't want to self-publish because they don't want to market the book. Sadly, no matter how you publish, you will be responsible for your own marketing. There are a very, very few exceptions, even with the traditional houses. It's true that when you self-publish, it's unlikely your books will be on bookstore shelves. But it's equally unlikely, if you publish commercially, that you'll be able to get bookstores to keep your book in stock beyond 90 days of publication. To sell your book, you need to find your audience, and write a book that resonates with them. There is no silver bullet.

Self-publishing will enable you to get a book out quickly, and to maintain full control and rights. You'll pay for that privilege, and it's easy to go wrong, but you can always make changes and adjustments as you learn more – which is not possible with commercially published books, because you no longer have rights to make those decisions.

Your Delicious Book

As you can tell, there are pros and cons with traditional publishing and self-publishing. Both options share the significant problem of limited marketing assistance. Either way, to have a successful book, you'll need to hire a pricey publicist or marketing consultant and make a significant time commitment to promoting your book.

I remember when my client Susan rattled off the number of projects she was in the middle of. I could see why she hadn't published her first book yet. Susan knows marketing, and she's not afraid to hire a consultant when it makes sense, but when it came to her book **Create Your Own Luck,** she was paralyzed. When we talked, she had already decided trying to get a traditional publisher was not a good option for her, but the effort to self-publish seemed massive and picking an author-funded press seemed overwhelming. It would have been very easy for her, in a state of overwhelm, to overpay or not get the results she wanted.

When it came down to it, the goal of the book was two-fold – secure press opportunities to build Susan's brand, and grow her subscriber list and fan base. On our consultation, we evaluated her options, and she decided publishing with Difference Press was the way to go.

Until now, if you want to publish a book, you've only really had two options – fight to get a publisher to sign you in an already crowded market, or pay tens of thousands of dollars to publish it yourself. The result is that many people give up – and great ideas go unshared. For those who do manage to sign with a publisher, the next steps pose an even bigger challenge – you are rarely supported or coached through the writing process, and months or years later when your book finally drops, the real test begins. Now that it's all done, will anyone actually buy it?

That's why I created the Your Delicious Book program. The program includes all publishing services with Difference Press, but you also get the strategy, coaching, editing, and marketing support from me and my team, to make sure you are writing a book that makes a difference.

Here's the deal. Author-funded publishers have a business model that revolves around getting clients, selling them a low-dollar package, and upgrading them once they are locked into the commitment. You could hand them the phone book, and they will publish it. They are a services firm and that's how they make money – they publish books. They don't care if you are making any kind of difference with your book. That's not what they sell.

On the other hand, traditional publishers do want you to make a difference, as long as that difference means lots of book sales. They only make money when you sell your book, and lots of it. So you write the book, you market the book, you sell the book, and they take 90+% of the revenue. Now there are advantages to working with a traditional publisher, and I have 2 clients (of the hundreds I have worked with) to whom I actually recommended this path. But for the most part, if you are reading this book, it's not for you.

I created Your Delicious Book so you could get all the services of an author-funded publisher, and all the strategy and emotional investment of a traditional publisher, that make it more likely your book will sell. Of course, the traditional publishers are investing it in *selling* because that's the way they make money, and author-funded publishers are invested in your belief that your work is worthy (even if it isn't) because that's how they make money. What we do addresses the weaknesses of both models.

THE DIFFERENCE PROCESS
STEP 9 – CREATE YOUR MASTERPIECE

So, how will you create your masterpiece? On the following pages are 4 publishing options. Review the pros and cons and select the option that feels best to you.

Need help? Feel free to schedule a free Strategy Session with me by emailing: info@TheAuthorIncubator.com or visiting https://yourbook.wufoo.com/forms/lets-get-your-delicious-book-written

Traditional Publishing

PROS	CONS
Advance payment of royalties	Low profit per book (5-8% royalty is standard)
Shelf space in brick-and-mortar book stores	Difficult to get a deal
Prestige and validation	Once you sell the book, you lose control over it
Help with getting reviews	Very little promotional help (beyond shelf space and review requests)
Introductions to book editors, proof readers, and people with marketing experience	Little incentive to promote the book yourself (since profits per book are generally less than $1.00)
No worries about design or formatting	Inflexible for future editions
Motivation and accountability	Deadlines which might not be convenient for you
Better access to mainstream media and conference speaker circuit	No control over cover art, back, spine, press releases, ads, or other media the publisher releases
Easy to get the book formatted, designed and printed	Self-published books can have a stigma for being unprofessional
No upfront money required	Need a platform to get a contract, but if you have a platform you don't need a contract.

Self- Publishing

PROS	CONS
Royalties between 50% and 80%	No advance payment
No approval process, you maintain complete control	Quality can suffer due to lack of expertise
Easy and flexible to make updates	No prestige or 3rd party validation
In the long run, it's cheaper to pay money upfront and get higher residual profits	Can be expensive depending on how much you outsource
You can always do a traditional publishing deal after	More work than just handing over a manuscript
No deadlines – work at your own pace	No external motivation
Total control over cover art, back, spine, press releases, ads, paper quality, and everything else	Bad distribution options is your book targets an older or less tech savvy audience
No agent needed	Limited opportunities to hit the big print best seller lists (e.g. New York Times Best Seller)
The time from proposal to 'go live' set by you	Takes time to figure out how to prepare, submit, and sell your books online

Author-Funded Publishing

PROS	CONS
Royalties between 50% and 80%	No advance payment. Significant upfront cost. And many author-funded publishers still take a chunk of your royalties
Experts managing entire publishing process	Very often you are sucked into an upsell cycle. If you don't like the work they produce, you have to pay more to see options
You don't have to tell people you are self-published	Harder and less flexible to make changes than with self-publishing
If you aren't super picky you can just hand over a manuscript and let them do the work	Probably locked into a contract so you can't transfer the book to a traditional publishing deal
No deadlines/ work at your own pace	No external motivation
No agent needed	Limited opportunities to hit the big print best seller lists (e.g. New York Times Best seller)
The time from proposal to 'go live' set by you	Once the author-funded publisher has your money they are actually motivated to LET you procrastinate. If you do, it saves them money. So your paid resource can work against you

Your Delicious Book

PROS	CONS
Write a book that will make a difference in peoples lives not sits in a box unread	Upfront investment required.
Develop a business plan to go with your book before you write it	
Tap into an active community of authors who are writing books that matter	
Have a publishing partner with experience to guide you through the process	Share control of design, timing and other aspects of publishing
Maintain 100% control of your royalties and your copyright	No special in-store display and promotional opportunities exclusive to traditional publishers
3rd party validation of an independent publisher	Can't do a traditional publishing deal with this exact book like you could if you self-published
Little work or learning curve about publishing and marketing	
Strict deadlines to provide accountability and motivation	Small fee for making updates after certain deadlines pass
Distribution deals with Amazon, Barnes and Noble, Kindle, Nook, iBook, as well as Baker and Taylor for in store orders	
No agent needed	
Relatively short time from proposal to 'go live'	Timeline not in author's control

High quality product

Help with marketing integration including advice on developing products and coaching packages that match with your book to defray book costs, establish passive income, and develop testimonials.

Limited opportunities to hit the big print best seller lists (e.g. New York Times Best seller)

INSIDE THE AUTHOR INCUBATOR:
ON DECISION MAKING

Q: I don't want to learn how to self-publish, and I don't want to wait for a traditional publisher, but I don't want to spend money to get published either. I don't like any of these options. What do I do?

A: When I'm really stuck and don't know what to do, I find that the best option is to do nothing. Make an active decision not to help people right now. Put your own needs first. You can hide from your calling for a while, but if it starts waking you up at night, you'll know it's time to make a move.

One of my clients was driving on a busy highway. She had been putting off signing up with me or doing anything in her business until she had more money. But the more she put off investing in herself, the more her clients were putting off investing in themselves. Even the meager rate she was charging was hard to get from her clients. Driving down the highway, she was thinking about how she was going to bust through this problem once and for-all.

That's when a 100 year old oak tree landed on her car. While she was driving 65 miles an hour! She couldn't see what was right in front of her.

Opportunity after opportunity had been coming and going but she was missing them. To get her attention, her Inner Author had to send a 2 ton slab of wood to do its bidding.

Believe me, if you are meant to write a book, your Inner Author will nag you until you do it. If you are *sure* you are supposed to write a book and just need help picking from among these options I recommend doing some muscle testing of the four ideas. Muscle testing is a form of applied or therapeutic kinesiology, which allows the subconscious to express itself by the strength of a particular muscle group, usually the shoulder of an outstretched arm.

In a standard muscle test, the person being tested or dowsed holds out an arm parallel to the ground and resists a gentle push downwards by a second person (the tester) with two fingers on the wrist area. This gives the latter a good idea of the base strength of the patient's shoulder muscles and allows any changes in muscle strength to be noted.

Have a friend serve as your tester. Once you establish the baseline, practice saying each of these sentences while the tester presses on your arm:

- I am publishing my book with a traditional publisher.
- I am self-publishing my book.
- I am paying an author-funded publisher to publish my book.
- I am going to be a part of the Your Delicious Book program.

Have your tester run four tests and compare them to the baseline. Notice during which of those 4 sentences your shoulder muscles were the strongest. That is your subconscious telling you what the right choice is for you. My friend Pam Slim has a great video showing exactly how the arm test works. You can watch it here: https://www.youtube.com/watch?v=xJp32Ycm7dM

Have a question for The Author Incubator? Send me your ideas, comments and complaints. I want to know what you think. You can reach me at:

www.TheAuthorIncubator.com/contact-us

CHAPTER TEN:
YOU CAN TELL EVERYBODY
THIS IS YOUR BOOK

Your income is determined by how many people you serve and how well you serve them...Your compensation is directly proportional to how many lives you touch.
~ Bob Burg & John David Mann, The Go-Giver

Most authors start by making their book idea as general as possible so it reaches the most people and sells the most books. Ironically, the reverse inevitably happens. In this information-overload era, more general info is not what's lacking. What's lacking is a heart-to-heart, soul-to-soul connection. There is another problem with that approach though – it's greedy. It might seem generous to you to say, "I want to help as many people as possible," but really that's your ego trying to cast as wide of a net as possible.

What if the net didn't have to be so wide, but instead, a tiny pebble dropped in the water and rippling out?

The servant-writer knows a book that really helps one specific person, and when that person reads your book, they become the second half of your broken heart locket. As you know by now, my process for writing a book that makes a difference has 10 steps. This step is the last – and it's all about going beyond the people who have the other half of the locket, and expanding your reach.

Some people will want to call this book marketing, but the truth is book marketing does not work if you have written the wrong book. Once your book has been written at least half of your marketing opportunities are gone: it's become too late or impossible to implement.

As we have established, the doorway to your ideal reader is through a problem. The people with that very specific problem will be the first to walk through the door labeled YOU. But then a funny thing happens. When you write a very narrowly scoped book like we have discussed here, with a universally applicable solution inside, your readers will figure that out, too.

This book could help so many other people even if they don't (have eczema, want to ask a girl out, like cheese, have the ability to make babies, etc.)!

What creates word of mouth power is when a reader has the intimate feeling that this author gets the problem, gets him or her as a person, and has a solution that he or she has been waiting for. Think about the books you recommend. I bet they are books that solved a problem for you. And I bet you recommend them to people who are not your author's ideal reader.

I've insisted to CEOs of Fortune 500 companies that they buy Martha Beck's book *Finding Your Own North Star*. I begged skinny girls to read Brooke Castillo's *If I'm So Smart, Why Can't I Lose Weight*. I don't even know you and I am pleading with you right now to go and purchase these 2 books. I posted something about it on Facebook the other day in fact and a half dozen people have emailed me to tell me they bought both books. I was so excited. I am an evangelist for these 2 women. And why? Because without them I am afraid I'd be 400 pounds, in a disastrous marriage, with a job I hated, and about a tenth of the income, luxuries and travel I experience today.

If you put me on the *Today Show* tomorrow morning, I would end up talking about these books.

This is how you can expand your market. Create raving fans. And honestly you don't need that many of us to dramatically increase the impact you make on the world.

But first, you need to serve like your life depends on it.

Have you read the book *The Go-Giver*? It's a really powerful manifesto about the power of service. In it the authors say, "Your true worth is determined by how much more you give in value than you take in payment."

Now let me just clarify, that doesn't mean you can't take payment. You can, and you should. Even if you don't need money to live, because you are the heiress to a great fortune, to serve you still need to charge people. One of the greatest gifts I give my clients is my willingness to steward their investments to make sure they reach the goals they set for themselves. I take the stewardship part very seriously.

But it starts with a servant's heart.

When I first started this business, I knew that I had a lot of knowledge about books. I had been helping authors create books for 16 years at that point. I wanted to give that knowledge to people. And, some people bought it. I was selling knowledge, and some people were buying. Yay! Sort of.

What I wasn't selling was *transformation*, and so I didn't have the opportunity to watch my clients transform. Everything clicked for me when I realized my knowledge was irrelevant if I couldn't get it to people in a way that turned them into bestselling authors that were changing the planet. What's worse, is without knowing it, I was actually contributing to the problem. I was helping my clients stay stuck!

When you think about the people you want to help, what is the transformation you want for them? Before you get all fancy with the Twitter handles and invest thousands of dollars with a publicist, answer this critical question.

Yes, there are lots of marketing tactics out there and some great strategies to get the word out about your book, and you'll find the right ones when you are ready.

Think you are ready right now? Then jump on a strategy session with me and we'll diagnose where you are at and come up with the best next steps. (You know the drill, email me at info@TheAuthorIncubator.com.) But make sure when you email me you include the info from the final step below.

THE DIFFERENCE PROCESS
STEP 10 – EXPAND YOUR REACH

How is your reader going to be different AFTER they finish your book? Think about your Ideal Reader Profile and list up to 10 results or benefits they are going to get from your book.

Here's my list:

- Write the book you were born to write
- Write with joy and ease
- Write a book you can use to grow your business
- Get your message out to the world
- Turn the pain you have experienced and the lessons you have learned into a format that can help others
- Create a lasting part of your legacy
- Build your credibility and confidence
- Make your friends and family proud of you

- Create raving fans
- Make the difference in the world you were born to make

Hey, you know what that is? That up, there – those bullet points – that, my friends, is marketing copy! But, it's not icky, slimy marketing copy designed to trick or manipulate people into buying based on inducing or avoiding a negative emotion. It's marketing copy that serves from the heart.

There are lots of books and programs you can purchase on how to market your book, but none of them will work if you don't start here.

Inside The Author Incubator:
On Marketing

Q: I hate marketing. Do I have to do it?

A: Nope.

But a quick follow up on that: Do you love the people you want to help?

Because if you do, you might not want to leave them suffering when you have the key to unlocking their pain. But you absolutely have the choice to be stingy with your gifts. Or not.

Have a question for The Author Incubator? Send me your ideas, comments and complaints. I want to know what you think. You can reach me at:

www.TheAuthorIncubator.com/contact-us

Conclusion

Because this business of becoming conscious, of being a writer, is ultimately about asking yourself, How alive am I willing to be?
~ Anne Lamott, Bird by Bird

Every book journey is unique but all of our authors share one thing, they have made their dream a reality by making the commitment and investment in getting their book done.

Difference Press authors share their message because that's what they were born to do. Writing is our tool, but changing the world is our mission. And we know we don't have to be ready or perfect to start making a mark, as long as we don't have to do it alone. As Anne Lamott also says on choosing the writer's path:

You are lucky to be one of those people who wishes to build sand castles with words, who is willing to create a place where your imagination can wander. We build this place with the sand of memories; these castles are our memories and inventiveness made tangible. So part of us believes that when the tide starts coming in, we won't really have lost anything, because actually only a symbol of it was there in the sand. Another part of us thinks we'll figure out a way to divert the ocean. This is what separates artists from ordinary people: the belief, deep in our hearts, that if we build our castles well enough, somehow the ocean won't wash them away. I think this is a wonderful kind of person to be. (Anne Lamott)

The Author-In-Transformation

- Knows they were born to write a book.
- Wants to write a book that will make a difference.
- Wants to feel safe, joyful, playful, connected and confident while they create their book.
- Isn't opposed to working hard or getting out of their comfort zone to get there, as

long as they know it's going to get done right.

- Is open to letting go of beliefs, stories, and patterns that have kept them from meeting their goals in the past.

It's hard to leave you here, knowing how many unanswered questions there are at this part of a book journey. That's right, every book is it's own journey and that journey itself is a gift you give yourself. You can tell yourself that writing a book is painful, and it sucks, and you will be correct. I've been on painful, sucky journeys though – like this one time in Wildwood, New Jersey, when my sister's contact lenses fell into a glass of Kool-aid somewhere on the boardwalk. Let me just say it was no fun. I'm more of a top-down, radio turned up journey girl myself. And if you want your book journey to go that way, you can choose it. Hell, I just did.

I wrote this book in two days. I started at noon on a Saturday, and finished at 7pm on Sunday. I got a full 8 hours of sleep. Had lunch with a friend. Talked to half a dozen friends on Skype and the phone. Played on Facebook, hung out with my cat, drank tea and wine. Even met with a client and a team member. I checked my email and played Words with Friends with my mom.

Don't let anyone tell you writing a book is hard. When you know how to nurture your Inner Author, you can write a book that transforms people's lives with joy and ease.

Acknowledgements

When I was growing up, this is how I thought the world worked:

1. Sometime between 12 and 16 years old you figure out what you are most passionate about in life.
2. Once you figure it out, you go do that and make lots of people happy and make lots of money doing it.

That's what my dad did, and I never really considered an alternative. In fact, I was 26 before I realized everyone wasn't madly in love with their job.

I am grateful to my father for modeling that life lesson and for teaching me always to autograph my work with excellence.

I fell in love with books long before I turned 12. I clung to the copy of *Frog & Toad Together* that Mrs. Sprouse gave me when I left her Kindergarten class and moved to a new house across town. I think that's when I learned books could be a port in a storm. Sleeping in a new bed, in a new room, in a big new house, the little 5-year-old me held fast to Frog & Toad till morning; knowing even if I didn't like my new school, I could always come home to my books.

My mom nurtured my love of reading and showered me in books for as long as I can remember. Thanks for saying yes to every Scholastic Book Club order with 50% of the books of the month circled, mom. You are the best! My mom is also my consummate editor and transcriptionist, with a good 30 years of experience under her belt and having her support means the world to me.

It was my friend Sue Philson who made me believe I was not just a reader, but a writer. Every girl should have a best friend as wise and kind as Sue when they are in high school. I am always grateful for the years of sleep-overs and adolescent Oprah analysis I shared with her. Without our friendship this book would not have been written.

It's no surprise to readers that my gratitude for the work of Brooke Castillo and Martha Beck runs deep. If you don't know their work, run – do not walk – to Amazon right and buy every book they have written.

I have had the good fortune of working with an amazing team at The Author Incubator: Jessie Sessions, Kate Makled, John Matthews, Alvin Ramirez, and Ann Alger have been instrumental in creating a safe space to nurture authors-in-transformation. I am grateful for their support, creativity and contributions. I would also be remiss not to acknowledge Dara Jones whose brilliant work with me early on in the creation of this company lead me to The Author Incubator name and to embrace the nurturing side of the work we do.

A word of sincere thanks to my mentor Kevin Nations, and the entire Kevin Nations FAMILY™ Mastermind group, especially Gary Henderson who inspired the creation of this book which had been brewing for longer than I care to admit.

And a final thank you to you! For believing in yourself enough to read this book. If you are reading this book, you are officially an Author-in-Transformation. What happens next – if you gnaw your way out of the cocoon and fly like the butterfly you are – that's up to you. But I hope you choose to fly. The world needs your voice.

About the Author

Dr. Angela E. Lauria is the founder of The Author Incubator and creator of the Your Delicious Book program. She has helped dozens of coaches write and publish  their first books, and has published books including Susan Hyatt's *Create your Own Luck* and Joe Mason's *Bankrupt at Birth*.

   She is the author of *The Difference: 10 Essentials to Freeing Your Inner Author & Writing a Book that Matters* (Difference Press, 2014), *If I'm So Smart, Why Can't I Be Happy* (Difference Press, 2013), and *From Medea to Media: Live Performance as a Vehicle for Social Change* (Atropos Press, 2009); the co-editor of *The World Almanac of US Politics* (Pharos Books , 1997); and an editor and researcher for *NIGHTMOVER: The Aldrich Ames Story* (Harpercollins, 1995), *Hong Kong 1997 and Beyond* (Summit Publishing Group, 1996), *Aboard Air Force One* (Fithian Press, 1997).

Her clients can be seen everywhere from O Magazine to MSNBC.com. Angela has a Ph.D. in Communications from The European Graduate School (EGS) in Saas Fee, Switzerland, and holds coaching certificates from Martha Beck International and The International Institute of Coaching Studies (IICS). She has spoken before audiences at the events including the International Coaching Federation annual event, Which Test Won? Marketing conference, Blog World, and Lean Start Up DC.

In 2011, the IICS named her their Empowerment Coach of the Year. She lives in Washington DC with her son and the world's hungriest cat.

About Difference Press

Built for aspiring authors who are looking to share transformative ideas with others throughout the world, Difference Press offers life coaches, healing professionals, and other non-fiction authors a comprehensive solution to get their book published without breaking the bank or taking years. A boutique-style alternative to self-publishing, Difference Press boasts a fair and easy-to-understand profit structure, low-priced author copies, and author-friendly contract terms.

Tackling the technical end of publishing

The comprehensive publishing services offered by Difference Press mean that your book will be designed by an experienced graphic artist, available in printed, hard copy format, and coded for all eBook readers, including the Kindle, iPad, Nook, and more. We handle all of the technical aspects of your book creation so you can spend time focusing on your business.

Over 20 years of experience nurturing books that make a difference

Founder Dr. Angela Lauria has been bringing the literary ventures of authors and personal coaches to life since 1994. You can learn more about Dr. Lauria's innovative approach to book creation or take advantage of a variety of free writing resources at TheAuthorIncubator.com

Your Delicious Book

If you're like many authors, you have wanted to write a book for a long time, maybe you have even started a book ... or two... or three ... but somehow, as hard as you have tried to make your book a priority other things keep getting in the way. Some authors have fears about their writing abilities or whether or not what they have to say is important enough. For others, the challenge is making the time to write their books or having the accountability to see it through to the end. It's not just finding the time and confidence to write that is an obstacle, the logistics of finding an editor, hiring an experienced designer, and figuring out all the technicalities of publishing stops many authors-in-transformation.

For more information on how to participate in our next Your Delicious Book program visit www.TheAuthorIncubator.com/delicious.

OTHER BOOKS BY DIFFERENCE PRESS

Woman Overboard! Six Ways Women Avoid Conflict and One Way to Live Drama-Free
by Rachel Alexandria

How to Heal Psoriasis from the Inside Out: An Energetic Perspective
by Marna J. Currie

Tapping into Past Lives: Heal Soul Traumas and Claim Your Spiritual Gifts with Quantum EFT
by Jenny Johnston

AGILE! The Half-Assed Guide to Creating Anything You Want from Scratch
by Sasha Mobley

Craving Love: A Girlfriend's Guide out of Divorce Hell into Heaven and a New Life You Love
by Shelly Young Modes

Dealing with Your Money Sh!t: Money Management that Focuses on Investing in Your Happiness and Creating a Budget to Attract Abundance
by Cassie Parks

Sex, Lies & Creativity: Improve Innovation Skills and Enhance Innovation Culture by Understanding Gender Diversity and Creative Thinking
by Julia Roberts

Mafia\Kitten: Lessons for Strong Women on Finally Letting Go, Feeling Safe, and Being Loved
by Valerie LaPenta Steiger

The Boy Who Became Father Christmas: The Story of Santa Claus
by James Wilmot

THANK YOU!

So… how observant are you?

I'm kind of a music nut, and I named my chapters after some of my favorite songs. Send me a recording (video or audio) of you singing any of the songs mentioned in my book (with your mailing address and permission to post it on Facebook) and I will send you a super secret, super special gift for you.

Couple other things in case you missed 'em.

FREE VIDEO CLASS: I have a companion video series that goes with this book. You can head on over to www.TheAuthorIncubator.com to sign up for it.

FREE STRATEGY SESSION: Wanna talk about your book ideas and get my take? Aweomesauce, let's do it! You can get started by filling out the form here:

yourbook.wufoo.com/forms/lets-get-your-delicious-book-written/

OR drop me an email if that's easier. I'm at info@TheAuthorIncubator.com.

FREE MUG: Ready to break from the chains of procrastination and writer's block? Declare yourself *Shackles FREE* with one of my gorgeous Free Your Inner Author Mugs. How gorgeous are they? Well you'll never know unless you:

1. Schedule a Strategy Session with me
2. Come to the Strategy Session with a copy of this book in hand, and ask about the mug thing.
3. Tell me the secret password when I ask (don't worry, I'll tell you how to find it).
4. Email me your mailing address.
5. Promise to post a picture of yourself drinking your favorite mug-friendly beverage on Facebook and declaring, "I'm Freeing My Inner Author!"